TExES Core Subjects EC-6 (391) Study Guide 2024-2025

Mastering TExES 2024-2025 with Comprehensive Study Material, Proven Strategies, Full-Length Practice Tests with Detailed Answer Explanations, and Expert Tips for Educator Standards Exam Success

Test Treasure Publication

COPYRIGHT

All content, materials, and publications available on this website and through Test Treasure Publication's products, including but not limited to, study guides, flashcards, online materials, videos, graphics, logos, and text, are the property of Test Treasure Publication and are protected by United States and international copyright laws.

Copyright © 2024-2025 Test Treasure Publication. All rights reserved.

No part of these publications may be reproduced, distributed, or transmitted in any form or by any means, including photocopying, recording, or other electronic or mechanical methods, without the prior written permission of the publisher, except in the case of brief quotations embodied in critical reviews and certain other noncommercial uses permitted by copyright law.

Permissions

For permission requests, please write to the publisher, addressed "Attention: Permissions Coordinator," at the address below:

Test Treasure Publication

Email: support@testtreasure.com

Website: www.testtreasure.com

Unauthorized use or duplication of this material without express and written permission from this site's owner and/or author is strictly prohibited. Excerpts and links may be used, provided that full and clear credit is given to Test Treasure Publication with appropriate and specific direction to the original content.

Trademarks

All trademarks, service marks, and trade names used within this website and Test Treasure Publication's products are proprietary to Test Treasure Publication or other respective owners that have granted Test Treasure Publication the right and license to use such intellectual property.

Disclaimer

While every effort has been made to ensure the accuracy and completeness of the information contained in our products, Test Treasure Publication assumes no responsibility for errors, omissions, or contradictory interpretation of the subject matter herein. All information is provided "as is" without warranty of any kind.

Governing Law

This website is controlled by Test Treasure Publication from our offices located in the state of California, USA. It can be accessed by most countries around the world. As each country has laws that may differ from those of California, by accessing our website, you agree that the statutes and laws of California, without regard to the conflict of laws and the United Nations Convention on the International Sales of Goods, will apply to all matters relating to the use of this website and the purchase of any products or services through this site.

Contents

Introduction	1
Brief Overview of the TExES Exam and Its Importance	3
Detailed Content Review	5
Study Schedules And Planning Advice	7
Frequently Asked Questions	10
1. Foundations of Literacy	13
2. Writing and Language Skills	21
3. The Science of Teaching Reading	27
4. Number Sense and Operations	33
5. Algebraic Concepts	39
6. Geometry and Measurement	45
7. Data Analysis and Probability	51
8. History and Government	56
9. Geography and Culture	61
10. Economics	65
11. Scientific Inquiry	69
12. Life Science	74
13. Physical Science	78

14. Earth and Space Science	86
15. Fine Arts	92
16. Health and Wellness	98
17. Physical Education	102
18.1 Full-Length Practice Test 1	106
18.2 Answer Sheet - Practice Test 1	130
19.1 Full-Length Practice Test 2	144
19.2 Answer Sheet - Practice Test 2	174
Test-Taking Strategies	187
Additional Resources	190
Explore Our Range of Study Guides	193

INTRODUCTION

Welcome to "TExES Exam Prep 2024–2025: TExES Core Subjects EC-6 (391)," a comprehensive guide meticulously crafted to empower aspiring educators on their journey towards triumph in the Texas Examinations of Educator Standards (TExES) exam. At Test Treasure Publication, we are dedicated to nurturing your success and guiding you toward an extraordinary future in education.

The TExES exam stands as a pivotal milestone for those aspiring to become certified educators in the state of Texas. This comprehensive assessment evaluates your understanding of the educator standards and your readiness to excel in the classroom. We understand the significance of this endeavor and are committed to providing you with the knowledge, strategies, and motivation necessary to conquer this challenge.

In the pages that follow, you will find a wealth of resources designed to prepare you for every facet of the TExES exam. Our approach transcends traditional study guides by acting as your dedicated mentor throughout your preparation journey. Whether you are a prospective educator, a career changer, or a dedicated teacher candidate, this book is tailored to meet your needs and guide you towards excellence.

Key Features of "TExES Exam Prep 2024–2025":

- **In-Depth Content Review:** Explore the core subjects of English Language Arts and Reading, Mathematics, Social Studies, Science, Fine

Arts, Health, and Physical Education. Gain mastery over key concepts and skills necessary for success.

- **Proven Test-Taking Strategies:** Uncover a treasure trove of proven strategies to tackle diverse question types with confidence. From time management to tackling complex scenarios, we equip you with the tools to shine on exam day.

- **Practice Makes Perfect:** Engage with two full-length practice tests, each containing 100 carefully crafted questions, reflective of the actual exam format. Detailed answer explanations ensure that you grasp the underlying principles behind every solution.

- **Motivation and Inspiration:** Journey through stories of success and perseverance that remind you of your potential to make a meaningful impact as an educator. Our final words serve as a beacon of motivation, propelling you forward with unwavering determination.

At Test Treasure Publication, we believe that every student has the potential to become an exceptional educator. Our mission is to provide you with the guidance, resources, and unwavering support you need to navigate the TExES exam successfully. This book isn't just about passing a test; it's about embarking on a transformative expedition towards educational excellence.

Prepare to embark on this enriching journey, where every page holds a gem of wisdom, every strategy enhances your readiness, and every practice question brings you closer to success. Your dedication and commitment are the keys that will unlock the doors to educator excellence. Let's embark on this journey together!

Brief Overview of the TExES Exam and Its Importance

The Texas Examinations of Educator Standards (TExES) exam is a pivotal assessment designed to evaluate the knowledge, skills, and readiness of aspiring educators seeking certification in the state of Texas. It serves as a fundamental step towards obtaining educator certification and plays a crucial role in shaping the future of educators in the classroom.

Exam Pattern:
The TExES exam is comprehensive and covers a range of subject areas, ensuring that educators are well-prepared to teach effectively across diverse disciplines. The exam pattern varies depending on the specific test being taken. It typically includes multiple-choice questions, constructed-response questions, and scenarios that simulate real classroom situations.

Number of Questions and Time Allocation:
The number of questions in the TExES exam varies by test, but candidates can expect a substantial number of questions to assess their knowledge in the relevant subject areas. The time allocated for each test also varies, reflecting the complexity and depth of content being assessed. It's essential for candidates to manage their time effectively to address all questions within the designated timeframe.

Scoring:
Scoring in the TExES exam is determined based on a candidate's performance across the various question types. Each question type is assigned a specific weight,

contributing to the overall score. The score reports provide valuable insights into strengths and areas that may need further improvement. Achieving a passing score on the TExES exam is a significant accomplishment, demonstrating the candidate's mastery of educator standards.

Administered By:
The TExES exam is administered by the Texas Education Agency (TEA), the state agency responsible for overseeing public education in Texas. TEA ensures the integrity and validity of the exam, aligning it with the standards and expectations of Texas educators.

Importance:
The TExES exam holds immense importance for aspiring educators. It serves as a benchmark to ensure that teachers possess the knowledge and skills needed to create engaging, effective, and impactful learning environments. A passing score on the TExES exam is a prerequisite for obtaining educator certification, enabling candidates to pursue careers in Texas public schools and contribute to the educational landscape.

Preparing diligently for the TExES exam is crucial, as success in this assessment not only opens the doors to a fulfilling teaching career but also positions educators to make a positive and lasting impact on the lives of students. The knowledge and expertise demonstrated through the TExES exam lay the foundation for effective teaching practices that inspire, motivate, and guide students towards academic excellence.

As you embark on your journey to excel in the TExES exam, remember that your dedication and commitment to preparation will not only shape your future as an educator but also contribute to the future of countless students you will inspire and guide.

Detailed Content Review

In the journey towards mastering the Texas Examinations of Educator Standards (TExES) exam, a comprehensive understanding of the core subjects is paramount. This section of "TExES Exam Prep 2024–2025: TExES Core Subjects EC-6 (391)" delves into each of the tested subject areas, providing you with an in-depth review of the key concepts, skills, and knowledge you need to excel.

English Language Arts and Reading and the Science of Teaching Reading: Unlock the world of language and literacy as you explore foundational concepts in English Language Arts and Reading. From phonemic awareness to reading comprehension strategies, this section equips you with the tools to promote literacy development in your future students. Understand the science of teaching reading, including phonological and phonemic awareness, fluency, vocabulary, and comprehension strategies that lay the groundwork for proficient readers.

Mathematics:
Dive into the realm of mathematics education, mastering the core principles that form the basis of mathematical understanding. From number sense to algebraic concepts, geometry, measurement, and data analysis, this segment ensures you are equipped to foster a love for learning mathematics in young minds.

Social Studies:
Explore the rich tapestry of social studies, embracing history, geography, government, economics, and culture. Discover strategies to engage students with

historical narratives, geographical landscapes, civic responsibility, and economic principles, empowering them to be informed and active citizens.

Science:
Uncover the wonders of the natural world through the science content review. Delve into scientific inquiry, life science, physical science, and earth and space science, gaining the knowledge to spark curiosity and scientific exploration in your future students.

Fine Arts, Health, and Physical Education:
Recognize the significance of holistic education by exploring the realms of fine arts, health, and physical education. Learn how to integrate creativity, wellness, and physical activity into your curriculum, fostering well-rounded individuals who are both mentally and physically healthy.

STUDY SCHEDULES AND PLANNING ADVICE

Creating an Effective Study Plan

Preparing for the Certified Nurse-Operating Room (CNOR) exam requires a strategic approach that optimizes your study time and ensures comprehensive coverage of the exam's content. This section provides guidance on structuring a study plan that suits your individual needs and schedules.

1. Assess Your Current Knowledge: Before you begin, take a practice test or self-assessment to gauge your knowledge. This baseline assessment will help you identify areas where you need to focus your efforts.

2. Set Realistic Goals: Establish achievable goals for your study period. Consider the number of hours you can dedicate to studying each week and how long you have until the exam date. Keep your goals specific and measurable.

3. Break It Down: Divide your study plan into manageable segments. Given that the CNOR exam covers seven sections, consider allocating specific time to each section, focusing on your weaker areas while maintaining a balance.

4. Consistency is Key: Consistency is critical for retaining information. Dedicate a consistent time each day or week for study. Regular, shorter study sessions can be more effective than marathon sessions.

5. Utilize Study Resources: Make the most of your resources, including "CNOR Exam Prep Book 2024–2025." Refer to relevant chapters and practice questions. Use external resources when necessary, such as online courses and practice tests.

6. Active Learning: Engage actively with the material. Summarize key points, take notes, and create flashcards or mind maps. Discuss topics with peers or mentors to reinforce your understanding.

7. Practice Tests: Regularly take practice tests to assess your progress. These tests will help you get used to the exam format, improve time management, and identify areas that need further review.

8. Adjust and Adapt: Be flexible in your approach. If you find that a particular study method isn't effective, don't hesitate to adjust your strategy. Listen to your learning preferences.

9. Review and Revise: Periodically review what you've studied. This reinforces your memory and ensures retention of key concepts.

10. Self-Care: Don't overlook self-care. Ensure you get adequate rest, maintain a healthy diet, and manage stress effectively. A well-rested and healthy mind is more capable of retaining information.

11. Simulate Exam Conditions: As your exam date approaches, take practice tests under conditions that mimic the real exam, including time constraints.

12. Seek Support: Reach out to peers who are also preparing for the CNOR exam or consider joining study groups. Support from like-minded individuals can be motivating and beneficial.

Remember that effective study planning is not a one-size-fits-all approach. Your plan should be tailored to your strengths, weaknesses, and learning style. Stay committed, maintain a positive mindset, and keep your eyes on the goal of CNOR certification. Your dedicated effort will be the key to your success.

Frequently Asked Questions

As you embark on your journey to excel in the TExES exam, you may have questions and uncertainties. We've compiled a list of frequently asked questions to provide you with clarity and guidance along the way.

1. What is the TExES exam, and why is it important?
The Texas Examinations of Educator Standards (TExES) exam is a comprehensive assessment designed to evaluate the knowledge and skills of aspiring educators seeking certification in Texas. It's a critical step towards obtaining educator certification and preparing to excel in the classroom.

2. How is the TExES exam structured?
The structure of the TExES exam varies based on the specific test you're taking. It typically includes multiple-choice questions, constructed-response questions, and teaching simulations that assess your ability to apply your knowledge in real-world scenarios.

3. How many questions are on the TExES exam?
The number of questions varies by test, but candidates can expect a substantial number of questions to assess their understanding of the subject areas. It's important to manage your time effectively to address all questions within the allocated time.

4. How is the TExES exam scored?
Scoring in the TExES exam is based on a candidate's performance across different

question types. Each question type is assigned a specific weight, contributing to the overall score. The score reports provide insights into your strengths and areas for improvement.

5. How do I register for the TExES exam?
You can register for the TExES exam through the official Texas Education Agency (TEA) website. Follow the registration instructions and deadlines provided to secure your exam slot.

6. Can I retake the TExES exam if I don't pass?
Yes, you can retake the TExES exam if you don't pass on your first attempt. There are specific waiting periods and retake policies outlined by TEA. Review the guidelines and prepare thoroughly for your retake.

7. How should I prepare for the TExES exam?
Effective preparation involves a combination of content review, practice exercises, and test-taking strategies. Utilize resources like our book to understand key concepts, practice with sample questions, and develop effective approaches to different question types.

8. What resources should I use alongside this book?
In addition to this book, consider using reputable online resources, practice test providers, and academic materials recommended by educators and professionals. These resources can provide additional practice and insights.

9. What should I expect on exam day?
On exam day, arrive early, bring required identification, and be prepared to follow all exam center rules. Familiarize yourself with the exam format and review any last-minute strategies you've learned.

10. How can I stay motivated during my preparation?
Maintain a positive mindset and set achievable goals. Remind yourself of your

aspirations as an educator and the positive impact you can make. Stay connected with supportive peers and mentors to keep your motivation high.

Remember that your journey towards TExES exam success is both a learning experience and an opportunity for personal and professional growth. The challenges you overcome in your preparation will equip you with valuable skills that you can carry into your teaching career.

1

FOUNDATIONS OF LITERACY

Phonemic Awareness and Phonics

Alright, folks! Get ready to dive into the wild and wonderful world of sounds and letters. In this section of our study guide, we're going to unravel the mysteries of how sounds and letters come together to create words that make magic happen. It's like discovering a whole new universe!

We start by talking about something called phonemic awareness. Basically, it's all about being able to listen to words and pick out the individual sounds, or phonemes, that make them up. Like, imagine listening to the word "cat" and being able to hear that it's made up of the sounds "k," "a," and "t." It's a pretty cool skill to have.

We're going to break down phonemic awareness like nobody's business. We'll teach you all the skills you need to know, from separating and blending sounds to playing around with phonemes and seeing how they fit into different words. These skills are super important for building a strong foundation in reading and spelling. Trust me, they're the building blocks of all the good stuff.

But hold on tight, folks, because we're not stopping there. We're also diving headfirst into the wild world of phonics. This is where letters start to shine, my friends. Phonics is all about connecting the sounds of spoken language to specific letters or groups of letters. It's like decoding the secret language of words!

In our study guide, we take phonics to a whole new level. We're not just talking about the basics here. We're going deep. We're exploring all the rules and patterns that make phonics tick. We're talking about things like consonant blends, vowel digraphs, and even those sneaky silent letters that like to hide out in words. No stone is left unturned, my friends.

But guess what? We're not just about theory here. We're all about bringing phonics to life. We've got activities that will get you engaged, exercises that will get you moving, and real-life examples that will show you how all this phonics stuff actually works in the real world. We use all kinds of different approaches, so no matter how you learn best – whether it's by hearing, seeing, or doing – we've got you covered.

And you know what else? We've done our homework. We've scoured the latest research and best practices in phonemic awareness and phonics instruction, so you know you're getting the good stuff. We want to make sure you're equipped with the right tools to make informed decisions about teaching phonics in the classroom. We're all about giving you the power to rock it as an educator.

Here's the thing, folks. Phonemic awareness and phonics aren't just isolated skills. They're the foundation for reading, writing, and language development. It's like they're the spark that ignites the fire of literacy. So that's why our study guide doesn't stop there. We're all about seamlessly integrating phonemic awareness and phonics with other important stuff like vocabulary development, fluency, and comprehension strategies. We're painting you a complete picture here, folks.

When you jump into our study guide, you're not just memorizing a bunch of rules and techniques. You're diving headfirst into a world of language, where every sound and letter has its own special place and purpose. We're guiding you on this crazy adventure, helping you master the sometimes crazy world of phonemic awareness and phonics.

So, what are you waiting for? Come on over to Test Treasure Publication and get ready for an epic journey through the world of sounds and letters. Let our study guide be your compass, leading you to success in the TExES Core Subjects EC-6 (391) exam, and more importantly, in your journey as an amazing educator who's going to inspire future generations to fall in love with reading and language. Let's do this, my friends.

Vocabulary Development

Let me take you on a journey, my friend. Close your eyes and imagine ancient civilizations, where the very roots of our vocabulary were planted. Picture yourself in the bustling city of Mesopotamia, where scholars painstakingly etched their spoken words onto clay tablets, birthing one of the earliest forms of written language—the cuneiform script. Can you feel the weight of their curiosity, their insatiable hunger for knowledge? These magnificent tablets bridged the gap between time and space, allowing ideas to transcend borders and generations.

Now, let's fast forward to lively ancient Greece. Here we meet the great philosopher Socrates, who saw language as a key to unlocking intellectual growth and self-development. Ah, Socrates and his disciple Plato, the pioneers of rhetoric. They showed us the art of persuasion, the power of words to move mountains. Can you hear the echo of their vibrant debates, their sharp minds clashing like thunder?

Moving on to the enchanting Middle Ages. Monastic schools became the very heart of learning, preserving and expanding upon the wisdom of our ancestors. And then, dear friend, a revolution emerged. In the 15th century, a man named Johannes Gutenberg invented the printing press. It was like a bolt of lightning.

Suddenly, books were within reach of the masses. Language became a beacon of enlightenment, lighting the way to progress.

And then, the Industrial Revolution stormed onto the scene, demanding an educated workforce like never before. Educational reforms roared, nurturing the minds of the future. Reading, writing, vocabulary development—all became soul-stirring missions. Public education dawned upon us like a radiant sunrise, promising a fair chance for all to enrich their vocabularies.

In the 20th century, a new generation of scholars emerged. They delved into the enigmatic depths of language acquisition, peeling back the layers of our cognitive processes. Lev Vygotsky gifted us with his theory of the zone of proximal development—a concept that highlighted the importance of guiding learners, providing them with support as they ventured into uncharted linguistic territory. And then, oh, the wonders of technology! The digital age arrived, igniting a fire in our hearts. Interactive tools, online resources—possibilities exploded, expanding our horizons for language learning.

Here we are, my friend, standing on the precipice of a globalized world. Effective communication is now more vital than ever. Technology has surged forward, bringing cultures together like never before. But with this newfound interconnectedness comes a challenge. Our vocabulary development must keep up, jumping over hurdles and seizing the countless opportunities that lie before us. So, in this fast-paced information age, it becomes absolutely necessary to equip ourselves with a versatile and sturdy vocabulary. Only then can we build bridges, foster true understanding, and navigate the intricate nuances of language in this ever-changing linguistic landscape.

As we turn the page, my dear friend, let us delve into the strategies and techniques that will empower you to expand your lexicon. But it's more than just acquiring words—it's about deepening your love for language, opening your heart to its incredible power. Our sincerest wish is that this chapter will ignite a burning passion within you for vocabulary development, unlocking doors to endless possibilities. So, let us embark on this mythical linguistic odyssey together, journeying through the annals of history to uncover the precious treasures hidden within the vast realm of vocabulary development.

Reading Fluency

Let's talk about the magical adventure of mastering reading fluency, my friend. It's all about diving deep into the essence of it. Picture this: reading fluency is like a symphony, where accuracy, speed, and expression all blend together seamlessly to create a harmonious masterpiece of words. It's not just about getting through the lines, it's about painting vibrant pictures in your mind's eye and unraveling the intricate layers of a story or grabbing valuable information from a textbook.

But, hey, let's be real for a second. Building reading fluency is a daunting task. It's like climbing a mountain. But fear not, because I've got a trusty guide for you – Test Treasure Publication. They're going to take us step by step through the whole journey, so we not only understand but also feel the joy of reading fluently.

Alright, buckle up, my friend. Step one: Phonics and Phonemic Awareness. This is where the foundation of reading fluency lies. It's all about understanding those nitty-gritty details of sounds. Test Treasure Publication will hook you up with the goods – study materials that'll rock your world. With interactive learning and mnemonic techniques, they'll train your ears to hear those phonetic patterns, making the words flow effortlessly from your lips.

Now, onto step two: Vocabulary Expansion. You know what they say – a rich vocabulary takes you places. And with Test Treasure Publication, you're going on a wild journey through the fascinating word-world. Their study guides will introduce you to captivating terms that will make you feel like you're painting a vibrant picture with every word. From everyday words to super specialized ones, you'll be building your masterpiece of fluent reading.

Step three is all about Comprehension Strategies. Reading fluency goes beyond just vocalizing words – it's about truly understanding and thinking critically about what you're reading. Test Treasure Publication has got your back with their awesome study guides. They'll equip you with an arsenal of comprehension strategies so you can extract meaning, make connections, and truly get to the heart of any text. It's like unveiling hidden treasures buried within the pages.

And last but not least, step four: Expression and Prosody. This is where you put the final brushstrokes in your reading masterpiece. Test Treasure Publication will teach you how to inject emotion, intonation, and rhythm into your reading. You'll breathe life into characters, convey nuanced meaning through your tone, and captivate anyone who listens. With practice, feedback, and the guidance of their expert educators, your words will create a symphony that resonates with anyone who hears it.

Listen, my friend, Test Treasure Publication believes that reading fluency is not just some technical thing, but a downright enchanting journey. So, as you dive into their study materials, get ready to unlock doors to a whole new world of words. Get ready to uncover the secrets of fluent reading and set out on a lifelong adventure of boundless possibilities. Together, we'll make words sing and bring reading to a whole new level. Let's light up the path to reading fluency and fling open doors to an amazing future. Are you with me on this extraordinary journey?

Comprehension Strategies

Listen up, folks! Let me tell you about Test Treasure Publication. We're all about getting you in touch with your inner comprehension guru and helping you read between those oh-so-cryptic lines. We get that comprehension is like a Rubik's

Cube, not a one-size-fits-all kind of deal. It's a whole complex process that requires some serious skills and techniques, my friends.

So, our journey to comprehension greatness starts with this thing called activating prior knowledge. Basically, we're gonna dig into your brain and find all the stuff you already know and have experienced. We're talking about forming connections and laying down a foundation for comprehension that's as sturdy as a skyscraper. By starting with what you already got up there, we're gonna blast off and get you on your way to a deeper understanding of the text.

Next up, hold onto your hats 'cause it's time for predictive reading, my friends. This is where you take all that prior knowledge you just activated and put it to work. We want you to make some educated guesses about what's gonna happen next in the text. Get all up in that narrative and let your imagination run wild. Trust me, it's gonna sharpen those comprehension skills like nobody's business.

But wait, there's more! We're gonna dive headfirst into the importance of visualizing during your reading escapades. Picture this - you're creating these vivid mental images in your mind as you read. It's like you're a magician, conjuring up a whole world inside your head. We're gonna guide you on how to engage all your senses and make the words leap off the page and into your heart. It's not just about understanding the text, it's about feeling it, ya know? This visualization stuff is gonna make you feel connected to that story or subject like never before.

Oh, and folks, get ready for some mind-bending questioning techniques. We want you to ask yourself all kinds of deep, thought-provoking questions while you're reading. Think Sherlock Holmes, but with a book in your hand. By digging into these inquiries, you'll unlock hidden meanings and take your understanding to a whole new level. It's like being the detective of comprehension, my friend.

But that's not all, oh no! We're also big on making connections here at Test Treasure Publication. We want you to see how the text relates to your own life, to other texts, and to the big ol' world around you. It's gonna give you a whole new perspective and make you an all-around comprehension rockstar.

Now, hold tight, 'cause we're just getting started. We're gonna teach you how to summarize info, capture those main ideas, and spot all those juicy supporting details. We'll even dive into the author's purpose and bias - we're not afraid to go there, my friends. And get this, we'll uncover the secrets of inference, critical thinking, and evaluative reading. We're here to equip you with everything you need to be a comprehension master.

Here's the thing, guys. At Test Treasure Publication, we're all about personalization. We know every one of you is unique, and you deserve some tailored guidance to unlock your full potential. Our study materials are here to empower you, to turn you into an active, curious, and critical reader who can conquer any knowledge mountain with confidence.

So, what are you waiting for? Join us on this epic journey where comprehension becomes your superpower. Get ready to unravel the mysteries of the written word and embark on a path to extraordinary learning. Test Treasure Publication is calling you to this mind-blowing adventure where comprehension opens doors and leads to sweet, sweet success.

2

WRITING AND LANGUAGE SKILLS

Writing Development

Welcome, my fellow writers, to this incredible adventure that will guide us towards mastering the art of writing. Together, we will explore the secrets of crafting well-written sentences, paragraphs, and compositions that will capture the hearts and minds of our readers.

Just like building a sturdy house, our writing needs a solid foundation. We will dive into the nitty-gritty of sentence construction, focusing on the importance of subject-verb agreement, sentence flow, and using different sentence types. With interactive exercises and easy-to-understand explanations, we will equip ourselves with the skills to create concise, coherent, and captivating sentences.

Once we have laid this strong foundation, we will venture into the world of paragraph writing. Let's remember that paragraphs are the building blocks of our larger compositions. Together, we will learn how to develop paragraphs that seamlessly flow, supporting a central idea. From crafting compelling topic sentences to providing strong supporting details and bringing it all together with a powerful conclusion, we will unveil the secrets to crafting paragraphs that are both persuasive and cohesive.

Now, my friends, it's time to take on the challenge of essay writing. We will immerse ourselves in different types of essays, unlocking the doors to persuasive, narrative, expository, and argumentative writing. Step by step, we will navigate the intricate terrain of essay structure, focusing on crafting strong introductions, developing insightful body paragraphs, and leaving a lasting impression with compelling conclusions. By mastering these skills, we will become adept essayists, ready to conquer any writing task that comes our way.

But writing is not just confined to the classroom; it extends far beyond those boundaries. We must recognize the power of effective communication in our interconnected world. That's why we will also dedicate time to honing our written communication skills in real-world scenarios. From crafting professional emails to composing formal letters and persuasive writing, we will equip ourselves with the tools to thrive both personally and professionally.

At Test Treasure Publication, we believe that writing is a profound journey of self-discovery. It's a place where our thoughts come alive on the page, and our voices resonate through the written word. With our carefully crafted study materials, we invite you to embark on this transformative journey, where writing goes beyond mere words and becomes a powerful medium for connection, understanding, and personal growth.

So come, my friends, step into the realm of writing development. Let us unlock the doors to endless possibilities together. Let Test Treasure Publication become your guiding light, leading you towards extraordinary success in the wondrous world of writing.

Grammar and Syntax

I've always been fascinated by the magic of words and how they fit together. There's something truly captivating about the way grammar and syntax work their wonders. It's like taking a journey through time, exploring the origins of language and how it has evolved over the centuries.

Picture this: we're going back to the ancient world, where grammar was the bee's knees of education. It was all about expressing yourself with eloquence and clarity. Those ancient Greeks, like Dionysius Thrax and Aristophanes of Byzantium, were like the rock stars of grammar. They came up with intricate systems to analyze and categorize how language is put together. From the sounds we make to the rules that shape words and sentences, they set the stage for the grammar we know today.

Fast forward a bit, and Latin takes the stage. It was the big shot lingua franca of the Western Roman Empire, and it left its mark on the romance languages we know today. Those fancy patterns and sentence structures in French, Spanish, Italian, Portuguese, and Romanian? You can thank Latin for that.

Then came the Renaissance, a time when grammar became an art form. Folks like Desiderius Erasmus and William Lily were all about refining grammar and making it shine. They wanted people to fall in love with language and use it properly.

But here's the plot twist: the printing press enters the scene in the 15th century, opening the floodgates for more written material. And that meant people started demanding standardized grammar. Enter Samuel Johnson, who made the first comprehensive English dictionary, and Noah Webster, whose dictionary became an American classic. They wanted to set the record straight and make sure we all knew the rules of English grammar.

In the modern era, we've had some heavy hitters in the world of grammar and syntax. Ferdinand de Saussure and Noam Chomsky, for instance, revolutionized our understanding of language. They taught us that syntax is a key player in how we all communicate with each other.

Today, grammar and syntax are like the superheroes of effective communication. They ensure that we can express ourselves clearly and precisely, whether we're talking or writing. And as educators, it's our mission to master these magical forces and pass them on to our students.

So grab your study guide, my friends, because we're about to dive deep into the world of grammar. We'll uncover all the secrets behind word formation, sentence structure, and even punctuation. We'll unravel the mysteries of syntax, learning how it helps us convey meaning and intent.

And as we become one with the incredible world of grammar and syntax, our own language skills will soar. We'll become language wizards, able to empower our students with the gift of effective communication. Together, let's embark on this thrilling adventure where words hold unlimited power and every sentence becomes a work of art. Let's unlock the key to connecting with others through language and building a future where words bring us closer together.

Language Conventions

Hey there! Welcome to this section on Language Conventions. You ready to dive into the fascinating world of language and all its magical components? Great! Because we're about to embark on an adventure that will take us from grammar to punctuation and everything in between. Trust me, it's not just about memorizing a bunch of rules and regulations. It's about truly understanding the beauty and complexity of language and using it to express ourselves with clarity and precision.

First things first, we're going to explore the enchanting realm of grammar. Picture it - we're navigating through a maze, encountering nouns, verbs, adjectives, and adverbs at every turn. But fear not! We're heroes on a mission to construct coherent sentences and bring our ideas to life on paper. We'll learn about the different parts of speech and how they contribute to creating meaning and structure.

Next up, we've got punctuation, our secret weapon for adding rhythm and cadence to our words. Think of it as the spice that makes our writing flavorful and exciting. We'll dive into the subtle nuances of commas, colons, and semicolons, mastering their usage to create the desired effect in our writing. And let's not forget about the magical roles of quotation marks and apostrophes - they help us attribute dialogue and indicate possession.

Once we've got a handle on the building blocks of language, it's time to level up our writing skills. We're going to dive into the art of crafting sophisticated sentences and paragraphs that flow seamlessly and captivate our readers. We'll learn how to mix things up with different types of sentences - simple, compound, and complex - to create engaging and dynamic prose. We'll also uncover the secrets of sentence coherence and unity, ensuring our ideas connect seamlessly and avoiding any awkward disjointedness.

Ready for the next step? It's all about paragraph development. We'll learn how to organize our thoughts and create a logical flow of ideas using topic sentences, supporting details, and smooth transitions. By the time we're done, we'll be masters of constructing well-structured paragraphs that grab our readers' attention and keep them hooked.

And finally, we're going to polish our language skills to perfection. It's time to focus on precision and clarity in our writing. We'll dive into the world of spelling, expanding our vocabulary and understanding the rules that govern correct spelling and pronunciation. We'll also explore the intricacies of word usage and vocabulary, so we can choose the perfect words to express our ideas.

This journey through language conventions isn't just about gaining knowledge and skills. It's about discovering the true art of expression and finding joy in the power of words. Together, we'll conquer grammar, punctuation, sentence construction, paragraph development, spelling, and vocabulary. With the trusty

Test Treasure Publication as our guide, we'll navigate these linguistic waters with confidence and emerge as masters of the written word.

So, my friend, are you ready to unlock the secrets of language and let your creativity and communication skills run wild? Let's do this!

3

THE SCIENCE OF TEACHING READING

Principles of Effective Reading Instruction

Hey there! Welcome to the first chapter of our awesome TExES Core Subjects EC-6 Study Guide. Get ready to dive into the fascinating world of effective reading instruction. Reading is so much more than just figuring out words - it's this amazing process that opens doors to imagination, knowledge, and personal growth. At Test Treasure Publication, we totally get how important it is to have strong reading skills, so we're here to give you all the tools and strategies you need to become an amazing reader.

1.1 Creating a Language-Rich Environment:

To really love reading, it's super important to have a language-rich environment that encourages both talking and writing. Surrounding yourself with books, conversations, and all kinds of literature exposes you to new words, helps you understand stuff better, and makes you think critically. So as you start this journey, dive into a world of words that sparks your imagination and makes you want to explore the endless possibilities hidden in the pages of books.

1.2 Phonemic Awareness and Phonics Instruction:

For little readers, it's all about building a solid foundation in phonemic awareness and phonics. These fancy terms mean you gotta know the sounds in words and how letters and sounds connect. Once you master this, you'll be able to effortlessly blend, break apart, and play around with sounds. And when you combine these skills with phonics instruction, you'll be a pro at cracking those tricky words and handling the challenges of written language like a boss.

1.3 Vocabulary Development:

Unlocking the world of reading is all about having an awesome vocabulary. As you learn new words, you're not only gonna understand stuff better, but you'll also be able to express yourself more effectively. So, dive into new words by seeing them in context, getting explicit teaching, and having fun with cool activities. Building up your vocabulary will totally help you understand what you're reading and succeed in all things literacy-related.

1.4 Comprehension Strategies:

Being able to understand and make sense of what you read is super important. Smart readers use a bunch of cool strategies to improve their understanding. They connect new info with what they already know, make pictures in their head, ask themselves questions, summarize what they read, and check if they really get it. By actively using these strategies, you'll deepen your understanding, remember stuff better, and develop those brain muscles that help you think critically - meaning you'll totally rock at school.

1.5 Fluency Development:

Fluency is all about reading smoothly, accurately, and with feeling. It's like turning reading into a piece of cake. When you're fluent, you zip through the words, say them right, and sound so natural. And guess what? When you do that, you'll improve your understanding because you're not stuck on how the words sound. You can focus on the juicy meaning behind them instead. So, practice reading the same stuff over and over, have someone read to you like a champ, and choose texts that match your skill level. Your reading speed, accuracy, and style will totally improve in no time.

1.6 Reading Comprehension Monitoring:

Smart readers get how important it is to keep tabs on how well they understand what they read. They stop and think about it, ask themselves questions, and change their approach if they're not getting it. This is especially crucial when you're dealing with tricky texts. When you take charge of your own understanding like this, you become a reading pro who can tackle anything that comes your way. So, hone those skills of reflecting on what you read and you'll be able to handle any text like a total boss.

By embracing these reading instruction principles, you'll become a lifelong reader who can rock the written word with confidence and excitement. Remember, reading is not just a skill, it's a whole new world waiting for your exploration. So, join us on this crazy journey of enlightenment and let's discover the joy and power of reading together with Test Treasure Publication.

Assessing and Supporting Reading Development

When it comes to figuring out how to help kids become better readers, we need to dive deep into the nitty gritty. Reading isn't just about sounding out words and flipping through pages. It's an intricate process that uses a bunch of different brain stuff. From the very beginning, when kids learn to identify and play around with sounds, all the way to understanding really complex texts, reading is a wild ride that keeps on going.

That's why our study guide is here to help educators in a big way. We've got a ton of tools and techniques for assessing students' reading skills. We know that every kid is different and learns at their own speed, so we've made sure to include all kinds of assessments that work for different learning styles. We've got the old school stuff, like tests and reading logs, but we've also got some cool new ways to see how well kids can actually read and understand things. With all these different strategies, educators can really get to know a student's reading style and give them the help they need.

Assessing is just the beginning, though. Once we know how well kids can read, we've also got a bunch of strategies for helping them improve. Our study guide is packed with techniques that have been proven to work. We've got lessons on phonics to get kids sounding out words with confidence, and we've got guided reading sessions to help them practice their skills. But we're not just about the mechanics of reading. We also know that it's important for kids to actually enjoy reading, so we've got ideas on how to get them hooked and create a positive reading vibe in the classroom.

But we don't stop at the classroom. We believe that supporting reading development is a group effort. So, our study guide is all about bringing everyone together – educators, parents, and caregivers. We've got tips for how to keep the lines of communication open and make homes a place where kids can thrive as readers. We've even got book suggestions and fun reading activities for families to do together. Because when we work together, amazing things can happen.

At Test Treasure Publication, we're all about being the best in the biz when it comes to helping kids become great readers. We know that reading can change lives, and we're here to give educators the tools they need to make that happen. Our study guide is like a treasure map, leading the way to extraordinary success in reading and beyond. So come join us on this adventure, and let's unlock the secrets of reading together.

Differentiated Instruction for Diverse Learners

You know, when it comes to teaching, we can't just treat every student the same. It's like acknowledging that each of us is our own unique person, with our own story and abilities. That's where differentiated instruction comes in. It's this educational approach that recognizes that our learners come from all walks of life, with different strengths, weaknesses, interests, and ways of learning. It's not just about sticking to one method for everyone and hoping it works. It's about giving teachers a whole toolkit of strategies to meet the diverse needs of their students.

And let me tell you, inclusive classrooms are vibrant spaces where all learners can flourish. Through differentiated instruction, teachers can adapt their teaching methods, the stuff they teach, and even how they assess, so that every student feels engaged and valued. It's about using different techniques to give students different paths to absorb, process, and show off what they know.

Now, you're probably wondering, how does all this look in an actual classroom? Well, it starts with really getting to know each student. We're talking about understanding their strengths, weaknesses, and how they like to learn. Once we get that intel, then we can personalize our teaching, meeting them right where they are and tailoring our lessons just for them. We can bring in all kinds of activities, materials, and resources that resonate with their unique interests and abilities.

But it's not just about what we teach, it's also about how students show what they know. We give them choices in how they demonstrate their understanding. Maybe it's a project, a presentation, or a good old-fashioned essay. We want to honor their different skills and talents, and let them take charge of their own learning. It's like we're saying, "Hey, you're in control here. Show us what you've got!"

Oh, and let's not forget about the power of collaboration. In our classrooms, we build a community where students work together, share ideas, and learn from each other. We encourage them to interact with their peers, do group work, and engage in activities that help them develop those all-important social skills. It's not just about individual success; it's about learning and growing together.

At Test Treasure Publication, we see differentiated instruction as more than just a fancy teaching strategy. It's an approach that recognizes the amazing potential in every learner. We want educators to join us on this journey of embracing diversity and creating inclusive classrooms where every single student can thrive. That's why we offer study guides, resources, and online materials to guide teachers through the ins and outs of differentiated instruction. We want to empower educators to become true champions of student success.

Because you see, by giving teachers the tools to differentiate instruction, we're bridging the gap between potential and achievement. With Test Treasure Publication by your side, you're not just preparing students for exams; you're setting them up for a bright future full of endless possibilities. So let's go out there and make a real difference!

4

NUMBER SENSE AND OPERATIONS

Understanding Numbers

Come on, my friend, and join me on a wild adventure through the ages. We're talking ancient civilizations, baby! Picture this: the Egyptians, rockin' their hieroglyphics and all, were onto something big with numbers. They knew that numbers were the key to keepin' track of their massive wealth, building those mind-blowing pyramids, and getting a glimpse into the mysteries of the cosmos. They were ahead of the game with this idea of place value, using different symbols to show the power of each position in a number. Can you believe it? They were onto the idea that where a number sits means something big.

Now let's zip forward to the land of ancient Greece. Grab your thinking cap because we're diving deep into some philosophy. These Greek cats like Pythagoras and Euclid totally changed the game. Pythagoras, a name that still rings through the math world, discovered some wild secret hidden in musical intervals. He figured out that the length of vibrating strings could create some major harmony, and his findings set the stage for musical scales and the study of number theory. It's like he tapped into a whole new dimension of numbers through the music in the air. Talk about a revolution!

But hold on tight, because we're about to blast into medieval Europe. Things were a little chaotic, what with all the politics and religious fervor flying around, but in the midst of it all, some serious number magic was happening. Scholars like Leonardo Fibonacci came onto the scene and turned it upside down with their ideas. Fibonacci dropped the bomb on those old, clunky Roman numerals and introduced this new concept called Arabic numerals. It was a complete game-changer, making calculations way easier and more efficient. Talk about a foundation-shaking moment in math history.

And then, my friend, we arrive in the Renaissance. Picture a seemingly ordinary world, about to explode with genius. Johannes Kepler, following in the footsteps of Nicolaus Copernicus, took numbers to a whole new level. He used them to crack the code of planetary motion, unveiling the secret symphony that governed the movements of the stars and planets. Just imagine how mind-blowing that must've been! It shattered the old way of thinking and opened up a whole new understanding of the universe.

But wait, there's more! Here comes Sir Isaac Newton, the visionary who took the mathematical framework of classical physics and flipped it on its head. His laws of motion and creation of calculus changed everything. We're talking a scientific revolution! This dude's discoveries led to monumental advancements and brought us even closer to grasping the magic of numbers.

And here we are today, my friend, standin' tall on the shoulders of giants. We've got centuries of wisdom behind us, just waiting to be unlocked. We're on the brink of diving into the mysteries of prime numbers, exponential functions, and infinite series. Trust me, this is way more than crunching numbers. It's about seeing the majestic beauty buried within their structure.

So, my dear reader, let's buckle up and embark on this epic journey of understanding numbers. With history as our guide, we're gonna unlock secrets and discover the endless potential that lies within each and every one of us. Are you ready? Let's do this!

Operations and Properties

Let me take you on a journey into the captivating world of numbers and their fascinating relationships. Imagine, if you will, a beautiful gathering of numbers, gracefully dancing together and joining forces to create something even greater. This is addition, my friends, the art of combining numbers and unlocking the secrets of numerical expansion. Each sum we create acts as a bridge, connecting these individual values and forming a unified whole. And here's the really cool part - the order of the numbers doesn't matter! It's like they have their own secret language, assuring us that no matter how we arrange them, their combined sum will always stay the same.

Now, let's switch gears and dive into the intricate world of subtraction. It's like being a magician, using our mental tools to uncover the hidden truths lying within numerical systems. With each subtraction, we peel back the layers and embark on a journey to discover the origins of the relationships between these numbers. There's this thing called the subtraction property, which is like a symphony of balance. It reminds us that subtracting a number from itself always leads us to a fundamental result - zero. It's like the numbers are whispering tales of harmony and equilibrium in our ears.

But wait, there's more! Let's venture into the realm of multiplication, a land of endless possibilities. Here, we have the power to expand, reproduce, and magnify numbers beyond their original form. It's like weaving an intricate tapestry of relationships, connecting one number to another as we multiply. And guess what? It doesn't matter how we group the numbers or the order in which we multiply them - the result remains unchanged! It's as if the numbers themselves are like guiding constellations in the vast sky of mathematics, showing us the way and revealing the underlying structure of multiplication.

Last but not least, let's unlock the secrets of division. In this enchanting realm, we dive into equal distribution and partitioning. Division empowers us to untangle the threads that bind numbers together and uncover their deepest relationships. We discover that division has its own amazing properties - multiplying by the reciprocal brings us back to the original number. It's like a testament to the harmony that exists within the world of division. And let's not forget about divisibility, where certain numbers can be divided evenly by others, opening up new avenues for exploration and understanding.

As we embark on this exploration of Operations and Properties, let us remember that these seemingly abstract concepts are the very foundations of our numerical universe. Through our careful study and curious minds, we will unravel the mysteries that dwell beneath the surface, emerging enlightened and ready to conquer any mathematical challenge that comes our way. So, my fellow explorers, let's press forward, driven by our thirst for knowledge and guided by the magical wonders that await us in the realm of Operations and Properties.

Number Theory

Prime numbers, my friends, are like those rare gems that only reveal themselves to those who truly seek them out. They're the rebel kids of the math world, refusing to be divided evenly by anything but themselves and one. And believe me, unraveling their mysteries is like cracking open a treasure chest full of mathematical wonders just waiting to be explored.

But here's the thing: prime factorization is where all the magic happens. It's like the distinguisher between prime numbers and those sad, composite ones. Imagine using a fancy old sieve, called the Sieve of Eratosthenes, to sift through a bunch of numbers and uncover those hidden prime gems. It's like finding buried treasure right in your own backyard.

And let's not forget about those divine little tools called divisibility rules. They're like mathematical superpowers that let us determine, with hardly any effort, if one number can be divided by another. There's a secret rulebook, my friends, and it holds the key to easily knowing if a number is divisible by 2, 3, 5, or 9. Armed with this knowledge, we become these all-knowing math wizards, effortlessly deciphering the divisibility of numbers and uncovering their deepest secrets.

Now, factors and multiples may not sound as exciting as prime numbers or cool divisibility rules, but trust me, people, they're the threads that weave the very fabric of Number Theory. Imagine these factors as the numbers that divide another number evenly, like tiny building blocks in a grand mathematical Lego set. Then there are multiples, those numbers that come to life when you multiply a given number by different integers. They create intricate patterns, these factors and multiples, like a symphony of numbers just waiting to be discovered.

And speaking of delicate expressions, let's not forget our old friends, fractions. They're these elegant little beings, expressions of numbers in their most intimate and precise form. We'll delve into their world of numerators and denominators, discovering the difference between proper fractions, improper fractions, mixed numbers, and even those reciprocal fractions. Armed with this knowledge, we'll take on fraction operations like adding, subtracting, multiplying, and dividing with the utmost precision. It's like dancing with numbers, choreographed to perfection.

So here we are, my fellow explorers, on the brink of a journey into the fascinating realm of Number Theory. We're about to unravel the hidden facets of numbers, peeling back their layers like a mathematician's onion. Each page we turn will reveal new revelations, propelling us forward into the breathtaking landscapes of mathematics. Together, let's forge a bond with the beauty and depth of Number Theory, navigating the intricate paths of prime numbers, divisibility rules, factors and multiples, and the elegant language of fractions. Let us set forth on this extraordinary expedition, where numbers hold the key to unlocking the mysteries of the world and shaping our very future. Are you ready?

5

ALGEBRAIC CONCEPTS

Algebraic Expressions

Alright, folks, buckle up! We're about to dive headfirst into the wild world of algebraic expressions. This stuff has been around for centuries, like a timeless tale woven into the very fabric of mathematics. People way back when were all about getting a grip on numbers and how they related to each other, and that's where this story begins.

Picture this: ancient Egypt. Ahmes and Ahmose were some brainiacs who used math wizardry to solve everyday problems. They scratched their ideas onto papyrus scrolls, giving us our first glimpse of algebraic concepts. They started using symbols to represent unknowns, like the math version of a secret code, to figure out linear equations.

Zoom ahead a few centuries, and now we've got the Greeks rocking the algebraic scene. Pythagoras and Euclid were the OGs, using geometry alongside algebra to express and solve equations. They were amazed by all the connections between numbers and shapes, kind of like those moments when you realize your crush likes the same music as you. Their work set the stage for future discoveries.

Now, let's fast forward to the Islamic Golden Age, a time of mind-blowing intellectual enlightenment. One dude named Al-Khwarizmi took algebra to new heights. His masterpiece, "The Compendious Book on Calculation by Restoration and Balancing," became the ultimate guide to algebra. He introduced algebraic notation and clue us in on methods for cracking quadratic equations.

Then comes the Renaissance, bringing Europe back into the algebraic game. François Viète and René Descartes were the big shots, making algebra even fancier. They turned it into a legit language of symbols and equations. Basically, they were laying the groundwork for the algebra we know today.

Rolling through the 18th and 19th centuries, a couple of math Gurus named Leonhard Euler and Augustin-Louis Cauchy cranked up the heat on algebraic theories. They were all about digging into complex numbers, logarithms, and exponential functions. Their work opened up a whole new world of mathematical beauty and set the stage for future math-heads to keep exploring.

As the 20th century roared in, algebraic expressions got a makeover to keep up with the science and technology vibes. Computers joined the party, and abstract algebra kicked things up a notch. Suddenly, we were diving into concepts like group theory, polynomial rings, and linear transformations. It was like discovering a secret math club with all kinds of cool puzzles to solve.

And now, my friends, here we are in the 21st century. This is our moment to shine in the world of algebraic expressions, thanks to technology and the wonders of the digital age. With just a few taps and clicks, we can dive deep into complex equations, play around with variables, and whip up stunning graphs of functions. The power to unlock the beauty of algebra is literally in the palm of our hands.

So, as we flip through the pages of this study guide, let's soak up all the wisdom and insights that smart folks have gathered over the centuries. Let's embrace the sheer beauty of algebraic expressions and discover the joy that comes from unraveling their mysteries.

Because, my friends, this isn't just about solving equations and crunching numbers. No, no! Within the realm of algebraic expressions lies the power to unleash our own limitless potential. It's like finding a hidden treasure chest buried deep within ourselves.

So, let's strap ourselves in and get ready to embark on this grand adventure. Test Treasure Publication is here to guide us, lighting up the path to extraordinary success in the mesmerizing world of algebraic expressions. Let's do this!

Equations and Inequalities

Alright, so get this: equations and inequalities have been around since way back in ancient Egypt, like 2000 BC. Those clever Egyptians were using basic math to solve linear equations. Can you believe it? They knew that math equations were the key to understanding the world and predicting the future. Talk about mind-blowing!

But it didn't stop there. Fast forward to Greece during the Hellenistic period, and you've got scholars like Euclid and Diophantus laying the foundation for algebraic symbols and variables. They started using letters to represent unknown quantities and even figured out how to solve quadratic equations. These dudes basically expanded the math world and inspired future math-whizzes.

Moving on to the Middle Ages, there was this awesome time called the Islamic Golden Age where math knowledge from all over the place came together. One guy, Al-Khwarizmi, refined and organized algebra. He came up with practical ways to solve linear and quadratic equations. His work, like the "Compendious Book on Calculation by Completion and Balancing," totally set the stage for the algebraic methods we still use today.

Then, in the 17th and 18th centuries, rockstars like René Descartes and Pierre de Fermat took equations to a whole new level. Descartes came up with coordinate geometry, connecting algebraic equations to geometric patterns. And Fermat? He made huge contributions to number theory and explored the properties of equations. These guys were pushing boundaries like nobody's business.

Fast forward some more to the 19th and 20th centuries. That's when everything got crazy advanced. With computers and fancy computational tools, mathematicians could solve super complex systems of equations and inequalities like it was nothing. It was a whole new level of precision and efficiency. And as the field evolved, new ideas came out, like the theory of inequalities. This stuff gave us a deeper understanding of the relationships between quantities and their limits. Boom!

And guess what? Equations and inequalities are still super important today. They're used in all sorts of fields like physics, economics, engineering, and social sciences. They help us model and predict things, optimize resources, and make smart choices. In a world that's more connected than ever, being able to work with equations and inequalities is a skill that gives you power to navigate all the complexities of modern life.

So, in this part of our study guide, we're gonna go down the rabbit hole of equations and inequalities. We're gonna take you through their history and give you all the tools you need to tackle even the trickiest problems. We'll teach you how to solve linear systems and understand quadratic equations like a pro. Get ready to uncover the mysteries of equations and inequalities and become a total math master!

Alright, let's embark on this journey together. We're gonna travel through time and knowledge as we explore the fascinating realm of equations and inequalities. We'll dive deep into this timeless discipline and unlock its secrets, so get ready to become a math genius!

Functions and Relations

Hey there! So, imagine this...you're standing in front of this super mysterious doorway. You know it leads to two different worlds, but here's the catch: each time you put something in, you get something completely different out. It's like magic, right? Well, that's what functions are all about. They're like these enchanting portals that take numbers and transform them into new values with this elegant harmony.

Basically, a function is just a fancy rule that connects inputs to outputs. It's like a secret language that only those in the know can understand. And don't worry, we're gonna crack that code and dive deep into the world of functions and everything they have to offer.

But hold on tight, because this adventure is gonna get wild. We're gonna unravel the tangled mess of notations, equations, and expressions. It's gonna be like untangling a massive web, but instead of spiders, we're dealing with numbers. And trust me, this exploration will give us the power to see the hidden patterns and connections between values.

Think of it like exploring different types of relationships. Yeah, just like how people have all sorts of different connections, numbers do too. We'll go from the simple, like finding patterns in numbers, to the more complex, like mapping out relationships on graphs. It's like peeling back the layers of a juicy mystery, uncovering the hidden beauty and truths within these relationships.

And here's the amazing part: functions and relationships are everywhere! Like, seriously, they're not just stuck in textbooks. They're part of our everyday lives, from biology to economics to physics. They help us understand the world and make predictions. So buckle up, because we're diving headfirst into the real-world applications of this math stuff.

By the end of this journey, you're gonna be blown away by how functions and relationships shape our world. We'll gain this incredible sense of wonder and appreciation for the math that's all around us. It's like unlocking the doors to new dimensions, where equations dance and patterns come alive. Mathematics becomes this mesmerizing symphony of beauty and truth, and we get to be a part of it.

So, are you ready to join me on this mind-blowing expedition? We're gonna develop skills like critical thinking, logical reasoning, and creative problem-solving. Together, we'll venture into the world of Functions and Relations, where the ordinary becomes extraordinary and math becomes the ultimate adventure. Let's go!

6

Geometry and Measurement

Geometric Shapes and Properties

Let's start by getting to know the basic shapes that lay the groundwork for all the fancy geometry stuff. The circle is where it all begins, with its perfectly symmetrical circumference and all those points that are the same distance from the middle. It's like the symbol of perfection and unity. And let me tell you, this shape has some serious math possibilities! You can measure the area of circular objects and calculate volumes of things like spheres and cylinders. All that practical stuff that architects, engineers, and designers use? Yeah, it's all based on the good ol' circle.

Now, onto the triangle. This shape is all about stability and strength. You got three sides and three angles, which give us the foundation for a whole bunch of geometric principles. Ever heard of equilateral triangles? They have sides and angles that are all the same, making them like the epitome of balance. Isosceles triangles, on the other hand, have two equal sides, and they're all about symmetry. And then there are those scalene triangles, with no equal sides or angles. They're like the shape chameleons, always changing it up. With these triangles, we can solve all kinds of calculations, like finding missing angles or measuring the area of weird shapes.

Now, let's talk squares and rectangles. They're all about stability and rigidity. You ever thought about how squares are like the embodiment of fairness and equality?

All those sides are the same length and each angle is right at 90 degrees. Boom, fairness achieved! Rectangles, though, are all about practicality. They come in all different lengths and widths, making them so darn useful. And these shapes unlock the secrets of perimeter and area, so you can figure out how much space you need for your fences, walls, or even the dance floor at a party.

Alright, get ready to have your mind blown by polygons. These shapes are like puzzles that challenge our sense of regularity and complexity. From the elegant simplicity of a triangle to the mind-bending number of sides in some polygons, they showcase the beauty of symmetry, angles, and vertices. Regular polygons, like pentagons or hexagons, have sides and angles that are all equal. They're like the kings and queens of mathematical wonders. But then you have irregular polygons, with all their varying side lengths and angles, making things a bit more complicated. These shapes show us that not everything in the world fits neatly into a uniform pattern. And when we dive into polygons, we start to understand things like tessellations and transformations, which let us appreciate the artistry of patterns and designs.

Now, brace yourself for the world of three-dimensional shapes. This is where geometry steps out of the flat surfaces and into the realm of depth and volume. We're talking cubes and prisms, with their sides that are all the same length and angles that are all right at 90 degrees. They give us the foundation for understanding three-dimensional reality. And let me tell you, their properties, like surface area and volume, open up a whole new world of calculations. You can figure out how much stuff fits in a container or how much space you have in a building. But it doesn't stop there! We also have spheres, pyramids, and cones to explore. These shapes show us the hidden dimensions within our three-dimensional universe.

After our adventure through the world of shapes and their properties, we come out with a new appreciation for how math connects to our everyday lives. With a solid understanding of all these foundational concepts, we can analyze, calculate, and truly appreciate all the intricate geometric structures that surround us. So let's keep that passion and curiosity alive as we continue our mathematical adventures.

Measurement and Data

Alright, folks, let's kick things off by diving headfirst into the wonderful world of measurement. We're talking about putting numbers to things and quantifying all sorts of objects and phenomena using those fancy standardized units. From measuring the length of a ribbon to the weight of an elephant, it's all about giving something a numerical value to represent its size or extent. And trust me, as we go on this wild adventure, you'll see that measuring with precision is an art form in itself. We'll learn how to pick the right tools and units for different situations, like true measurement masters.

But hold on tight, because accurate measurements aren't just about math. Oh no, they go way beyond that and touch practically every part of our lives. Think about it: engineers need precise measurements to construct sturdy buildings that can withstand anything. Scientists rely on measurements to back up their theories with hard, empirical evidence. Even pharmacists count on measurements to mix up just the right dose of medicine to help ease our ailments. So, my friends, measurement is the universal language that connects us all. And when you understand its principles, you're armed with the power to make a meaningful difference in this crazy world.

Alright, let's shift gears a bit and plunge into the fascinating realm of data analysis. This is where we turn raw information into knowledge and insights that'll blow your mind. In this age driven by mountains of data, being able to make sense of it all is a skill worth having. It's like being a detective, peeling back the layers to uncover patterns, trends, and relationships that shape our understanding of the world and guide our decisions.

But how do we even start that detective work? Well, statistical analysis is our trusty sidekick. It helps us gather, organize, and interpret all that data to draw some serious conclusions. And hey, we can't forget about data representation. Graphs and charts are like the superheroes of visuals, letting us present information in a way that's both stylish and informative. Plus, we'll dig into concepts like central tendency and variability. They may sound intimidating, but they're like secret weapons that help us summarize and analyze data sets like pros.

But wait, there's more! We're not done yet. We're about to dive into a whole new dimension—probability. Now, this branch of mathematics is all about predicting and understanding uncertainties. It gives us the power to put a number on the likelihood of something happening. And let me tell you, that's a powerful tool for decision-making and risk assessment. When we understand probability, we can make smart choices, evaluate the uncertainties that life throws at us, and navigate this ever-changing world with confidence.

So, my friends, strap yourselves in and get ready for the ride of your life. We're about to embark on an exhilarating journey through measurement and data—an adventure that'll not only boost your math skills, but also sharpen your analytical thinking. You'll become a force to be reckoned with, equipped to make evidence-based decisions and contribute to the betterment of society.

Sounds pretty awesome, right? We're about to unlock a whole new world of knowledge, empowering ourselves and future generations with the stuff that can make tomorrow even brighter. So get on board and let's uncover the mysteries of the numbers that surround us. We're about to discover hidden treasures, my friends. Are you ready? Let's get this party started!

Geometric Transformations

Hey there, welcome to the fascinating world of geometric transformations! Get ready to dive into a world where shapes go through mind-bending changes, angles come alive, and polygons groove together in beautiful harmony. This journey is gonna stretch your imagination, give your brain a workout, and ignite your curiosity like never before.

To really grasp the significance of geometric transformations, we gotta take a trip back in time. Let's start in ancient Greece, where brilliant mathematicians like Euclid and Pythagoras laid the groundwork for this mind-blowing field. Euclid, the geometry guru, introduced the concepts of congruence and similarity, while Pythagoras blew minds with his epic theorem that showed the relationship between shapes and their dimensions.

Fast forward to the Renaissance, where artistic geniuses like Leonardo da Vinci and Albrecht Dürer took geometric transformations and turned them into stunning visual masterpieces. They played around with reflection, rotation, translation, and dilation to create mind-bending symmetries and illusions that blurred the line between art and math.

As we get closer to the present, the influence of geometric transformations becomes even more apparent in computer science and engineering. Just think about computer graphics – they rely on transformation matrices to make three-dimensional worlds look real and take us on virtual adventures that blow our minds.

Now, you might be wondering, what exactly are geometric transformations? Well, at their core, these transformations are all about changing the shape, position, or size of a figure while keeping its important stuff intact. It can be as simple as sliding a shape along an axis or as mind-boggling as a mix of rotations and reflections that produce intricate patterns. They allow us to tap into the infinite possibilities hidden in the world of shapes.

In this chapter, we're gonna dive deep into the different types of geometric transformations. We'll explore their properties, characteristics, and how they're practically used. Get ready for some hands-on fun as we bring these transformations to life through interactive games, eye-catching visuals, and examples that hit close to home.

But we're not stopping at just the mechanics. We'll also dig into the concepts of symmetry, congruence, and similarity, and how they're all connected to our everyday lives. From the mind-blowing symmetries found in nature to the genius engineering inspired by similar shapes, we're gonna unlock the true power of geometric transformations as a tool to understand and interpret the world around us.

So, my friend, buckle up and get ready for an epic journey through the universe of geometric transformations. Each chapter will unlock new insights, broaden your understanding, and set you on the path to becoming a master. Together, let's uncover the endless possibilities that lie within the magical world of shapes and their incredible transformations.

7

DATA ANALYSIS AND PROBABILITY

Data Interpretation

Let's go on a little adventure, back in time to the days of ancient civilizations. Picture yourself in the beautiful city of Babylon, nestled by the flowing Tigris and Euphrates rivers. In this ancient city, a bunch of scribes painstakingly wrote down all sorts of things on clay tablets – from business transactions to inventories to even observations of the stars. Can you imagine? These ancient records show how our ancestors were always hungry to understand the world around them, always searching for meaning in all that data.

Now, fast forward to the Renaissance period. Ahh, what a golden age of curiosity and innovation! Imagine hanging out with creative geniuses like Leonardo da Vinci and Galileo Galilei. Together, they revolutionized the way we look at and make sense of data. Their crazy experiments and observations paved the way for the scientific method, turning data from just random observations into something much more valuable – evidence and knowledge.

Alright, now let's zoom ahead again, this time to the Industrial Revolution. Woah, hold on tight because things are about to get wild! With this revolution came a massive explosion of data. The world was changing so fast, with incredible advancements in technology and the collection of information. And guess what? That led to the birth of modern statistics! Suddenly, scientists and researchers had this amazing tool to make groundbreaking discoveries and unlock all the mysteries of the world. How cool is that?

But wait, there's more! We're now in the digital age, and oh boy, things are getting even crazier. The volume and complexity of data are exploding at an insane rate. We're standing right at the cutting edge of a data-driven era, where information is like a key that can unlock infinite possibilities. Seriously, data interpretation is the name of the game these days, no matter what field you're in – healthcare, finance, marketing, you name it. As the world becomes increasingly connected, the ability to analyze and interpret loads of data becomes seriously important.

Now, in this part of our study guide, we're gonna give you all the tools, strategies, and techniques you need to navigate through the twists and turns of data interpretation. We're gonna take you from just understanding the basics of statistics to diving deep into deciphering those complicated data sets you've been scratching your head over. It's gonna be a wild ride, but don't worry, we're right here with you every step of the way.

Together, we'll explore all sorts of cool ways to visualize data, like graphs, charts, and tables. These are like magic tricks that can make even the most complicated information seem simple and reveal some seriously amazing insights. We'll also dive into the world of probability and statistics – you know, those hidden patterns and correlations that are lurking within the data, just waiting for us to discover them.

But here's the thing – data interpretation isn't just about crunching numbers. It's a whole lot more than that. It takes critical thinking, problem-solving skills, and the ability to draw logical conclusions. We're gonna guide you through the whole process of analyzing data critically, and making sure you spot any biases or flaws in the way it was collected. We want you to be able to draw accurate and well-informed conclusions – the kind that are backed up by solid evidence.

So, are you ready for this thrilling journey? Remember, data interpretation isn't just a skill for some test – it's a skill for life. It's gonna empower you to make informed decisions and challenge the things that everyone else thinks they know. Trust us, it's gonna be a wild ride filled with surprises. It's gonna take you beyond the ordinary and help you achieve some seriously extraordinary things.

So, what do you say? Let's unlock the mysteries of data interpretation together. Let's show the world how the world of numbers is like a giant canvas, just waiting for you to create, analyze, and interpret your very own masterpiece. Come on, join us on this adventure, and let's embrace the power of data. It's gonna be something you won't forget!

Probability Concepts

You know what's fascinating? Probability. It's this crazy concept that shows up in all sorts of math and science stuff. It's like a little window into the world of uncertainty and chance, giving us a sneak peek at what might happen in the future. Super cool, right?

So, in this part of our study guide, we're gonna dive headfirst into the world of probability. We're gonna uncover all its secrets and give you the tools to navigate through all the craziness with confidence. 'Cause let's face it, life is uncertain, and being able to make informed predictions and decisions is pretty important.

We at Test Treasure Publication believe that probability is, like, the foundation for success in all sorts of academic and everyday stuff. From crunching numbers to making smart money moves, probability is everywhere. That's why we've put together a comprehensive breakdown of all the key concepts you need to know. We've got your back, my friend.

Alright, let's start with the basics. We gotta understand that the future is never certain. There are always a bunch of different outcomes for any event, and that's where probability comes in. It helps us figure out how likely each outcome is. Sounds useful, right? You betcha.

Now that we've got that down, let's move on to the fun stuff. We're gonna explore probability distributions, which is just a fancy way of saying we're gonna analyze random variables and their probabilities. We'll learn all about the difference between discrete and continuous distributions, and how to calculate probabilities using all sorts of fancy functions.

Next up, it's time to talk about conditional probability. This is when we gotta figure out the likelihood of one event happening if something else has already happened. It's a big deal in real life, 'cause sometimes one thing affects what happens next. Gotta be ready for those twists and turns, my friend.

But wait, there's more! We're gonna dive into the world of combinatorics and permutations. Hold on, it's not as scary as it sounds. These concepts just help us count all the different outcomes and arrangements in situations with lots of possibilities. Like, think of it as figuring out how many different ways a game can play out or the chances of a specific combo happening.

And if that's not enough, we're gonna talk about something called expected value. Basically, it helps us figure out the average outcome of a random variable. It comes in handy when we gotta make the best decision based on all the possible outcomes and their probabilities.

Last but not least, we're gonna wrap things up with probability models and simulations. These are like our super tools for estimating the likelihood of certain events based on stats and computer magic. We'll explore different models, like binomial, geometric, and Poisson distributions, and learn how to use simulations to make those probability predictions.

By the time you finish up this section, you're gonna be a probability pro. Our explanations, examples, and practice problems are gonna make it all crystal clear, trust me. You'll be able to handle any probability question that comes your way. We've got your back, my friend.

At Test Treasure Publication, we're all about making things easy to understand. Probability's no exception. Our goal is to give you the tools and resources to be your best self and succeed in all your academic adventures. So come join us in the exciting world of probability. It's gonna sharpen your brain and open doors to endless possibilities. Let's do this!

8

HISTORY AND GOVERNMENT

Historical Events and Concepts

Picture this: a journey back in time, where we step foot into the mysterious lands of ancient civilizations like Egypt, Mesopotamia, Greece, and Rome. We're talking about the very foundations of Western civilization here! Imagine standing in front of the towering pyramids of Giza, their majesty taking your breath away. And let's not forget about those ancient Greek thinkers, deep in philosophical musings that still make our heads spin today. Oh, and the rise and fall of the mighty Roman Empire? It's like watching a dramatic saga unfold before our eyes.

Fast forward a bit, and now we're in the Middle Ages and the Renaissance. Feudalism is on the rise, Christianity is spreading like wildfire, and powerful empires like the Byzantine Empire and the Holy Roman Empire are flexing their muscles. But here's where things get really interesting: the Renaissance. This is the time when art, science, and intellectual exploration explode onto the scene. We're talking about the likes of Leonardo da Vinci and Michelangelo, people who changed the world with their sheer talent and creativity. And let's not forget about the Protestant Reformation, a time of intense religious conflict that reshaped Europe forever.

Now, hold on tight because we're boarding a ship and sailing across vast oceans. Picture explorers like Christopher Columbus, Vasco da Gama, and Ferdinand

Magellan, braving the unknown in search of new trade routes and untold riches. But here's the kicker: their explorations led to something much bigger. It led to colonization. Empires expanded their territories, leaving lasting impacts on indigenous cultures and economies. It was a collision of civilizations, the New World meeting the Old in a clash that changed everything.

Next up, we have the Enlightenment and the French Revolution. This is the time when reason and individual rights started to challenge traditional authority. Think of philosophers like John Locke, Voltaire, and Jean-Jacques Rousseau, shaking things up with their radical ideas. And then, the French Revolution comes roaring in, shaking the very foundation of monarchy and aristocracy. It's history in the making, my friend.

But wait, there's more! Buckle up because we're about to witness the Industrial Revolution, a time of mind-boggling technological advancements, cities springing up left and right, and society undergoing massive changes. Picture factories churning out goods, railways weaving their way across landscapes, and an entirely new way of life emerging. It was the birth of modern economies as we know them.

And speaking of change, globalization took center stage. Suddenly, our world became more interconnected than ever before. Trade, information, and cultural exchange transformed the way we lived. It was like an invisible web, connecting people from opposite corners of the globe.

But it wasn't all sunshine and rainbows. The 20th century brought us not one, but two devastating world wars. Nations were tested, politics were reshaped, and the scars still remain. World War I led to the rise of totalitarian regimes, setting the stage for World War II. And if that wasn't enough, we had the Cold War, a tense power struggle between the United States and the Soviet Union that shaped the world for decades. It was a time of fear, uncertainty, and a constant state of unease.

But amidst all the darkness, there were flickers of hope. The fight for civil rights and equality gained momentum, with marginalized communities rising up against discrimination, racism, and injustice. From the African American Civil Rights Movement to the feminist movement and the LGBTQ+ rights movement, change was in the air. We were witnessing history in the making, my friend.

And here we are, in the new millennium. Technology and globalization have taken us to new heights, both challenging and opening up new opportunities. Our world has become more interconnected and complex, presenting us with endless possibilities. It's a time to reflect on how far we've come and the journey that lies ahead.

So, my fellow time travelers, as we delve into the depths of history, we're not just studying events and concepts. We're uncovering the very essence of what it means to be human. We're immersing ourselves in the rich tapestry of social, political, and cultural dynamics that have shaped our world. Together, we're embarking on a transformative journey, one that will forever alter your perspective and equip you with the knowledge and insights needed to conquer the TExES Core Subjects EC-6 exam and thrive in your future teaching career.

Now, are you ready to dive deep into the past and explore the incredible human experience? Let's go!

Civic Participation and Government

Hey there! Welcome to Chapter 7 of the TExES Core Subjects EC-6 (391) Study Guide. We're diving headfirst into the amazing world of civic participation and government, where individuals like you and me have the power to shape the destiny of our society. Get ready for an exciting journey that'll not only help you understand the ins and outs of government but also empower you to actively participate in the democratic process.

Section 1: Understanding Government

In this section, we're laying the foundation for your understanding of government. We're exploring all kinds of governments, from fancy monarchies to good ol' democracies, and the different systems that impact the lives of individuals worldwide. Get ready for some mind-boggling discussions as we unravel the complexities of governmental structures and dig into the roles of key institutions like the executive, legislative, and judicial branches.

Section 2: The Importance of Civic Participation

Now that we've got a solid understanding of government, it's time to dig into the significance of civic participation. This section is all about the fundamental principles of democracy and why us citizens play a crucial role in shaping public policy. We won't bore you with textbook stuff, oh no! Instead, we'll grab your attention with riveting case studies and real-world examples that'll open your eyes to the power of collective action and grassroots movements. From voting to community organizing, we've got all the tools you need to become an active and engaged citizen.

Section 3: Advocacy and Activism

Building on the concept of civic participation, Section 3 is taking us on a wild exploration of advocacy and activism. We're diving into the different strategies used to bring about social and political change. Get ready for a rollercoaster ride of peaceful protests and epic lobbying efforts. We'll even dive into the power of persuasion and the role of media in shaping public opinion. And hey, who doesn't love interactive activities? So get ready to develop some kickass skills like effective communication and critical thinking. You'll be a powerhouse advocate for causes that truly matter to you.

Section 4: Local Government and Community Engagement

Now let's zoom in on the importance of local government and community engagement. We'll uncover how local governments operate and what their role is in providing essential services to our communities. You'll also get a taste of how you can get involved in local governance, from attending city council meetings to stepping up and volunteering for community initiatives. Brace yourself for some mind-blowing case studies and interactive exercises that'll show you just how much of a meaningful impact you can make in your own neighborhood.

Section 5: Social Responsibility and Ethical Decision-Making

In this final section of our adventure, we're diving deep into the core values of social responsibility and ethical decision-making. As individuals, we have a responsibility to our communities and the wider world. So get ready for some thought-provoking discussions and ethical dilemmas that'll make your brain do flips. We'll explore how our personal values and societal norms intersect and influence our decision-making processes. By understanding the true consequences of our choices, we can make sure our actions align with the greater good.

Conclusion:

Woohoo! You made it through Chapter 7: Civic Participation and Government. Armed with a comprehensive understanding of government structures, the importance of civic participation, and all the neat tools of advocacy and activism, you're well on your way to becoming an empowered citizen. So remember, my friend, the power to shape the world around us lies within each and every one of us. Embrace that responsibility and dive into the democratic process with all the passion and dedication in your heart. Together, we can create a brighter and more just future for all.

9

GEOGRAPHY AND CULTURE

Geographic Regions and Features

1. Let me take a moment to break down the whole idea of geographic regions for you. These regions are like puzzle pieces that help us understand the world better. They bring together areas that share similar physical features, cultural vibes, or environmental characteristics. Think of it like this: towering mountains, vast deserts, stunning coastlines, and thick forests all have their own unique flair.

2. Now, let's talk about those jaw-dropping mountains. We're talking about majestic ranges that dominate the landscape on a global scale. Picture yourself standing at the base of the mighty Himalayas. Those snow-capped peaks seem like they're reaching for the heavens, almost beckoning you to come closer. Or maybe you can feel the wild energy coursing through your veins as you stand in the midst of the Rocky Mountains in North America. From the Andes in South America to the Alps in Europe, every mountain range is a thrilling glimpse into nature's power.

3. Brace yourself for a journey into the enigmatic world of deserts. Get ready to be blown away by the immensity and solitude these places offer. Just close your eyes and imagine walking through the shifting sands of the Sahara. The golden hues stretch beyond the imagination, and it feels like you're surrounded by nothingness. Let the Mojave Desert in North America cast its spell on you. The

land is bone-dry, painted in mute shades, but it still manages to captivate even the most seasoned travelers. Deserts, with their extreme climates and unique plants and animals, teach us a thing or two about resilience in the face of adversity.

4. Now, let's dive into the mysteries of water. Get ready to explore the vast oceans, seas, lakes, and rivers that make up our watery wonders. Just stand by the breathtaking Pacific Ocean and listen to those waves crashing against the shore. It's like a lullaby of nature, soothing your soul. And then, picture yourself sailing on the mighty Amazon River, winding your way through lush rainforests. Oh, and don't forget to marvel at the Great Barrier Reef, with its otherworldly beauty. Underneath those crystal-clear waters, you'll see coral formations dancing in vibrant colors. These bodies of water are teeming with life, shaping the world's ecosystems and impacting our lives in countless ways.

5. Alright, folks, it's time to embrace the diversity of forests. Take a deep breath and let the symphony of rustling leaves and chirping birds guide us into the heart of these beautiful wooded realms. Venture into the Amazon Rainforest, where the colors and ancient secrets overflow in every corner. Or imagine yourself in the mystical taiga of Siberia, surrounded by sturdy spruce and fir trees that stand tall against the winter winds. These forests are the epitome of life's variety and natural harmony. Take a closer look at the incredible adaptations of the plants and animals that call these forests home. You'll witness the delicate balance between humans and the preservation of these incredible treasures.

Now that we've covered all the amazing geographic regions, let's pause for a moment and reflect on their impact on our lives. It's not just about their beauty or the amazing experiences they offer to those who venture into them. These regions shape our climate, influence our cultures, and provide invaluable resources. By understanding and appreciating these connections, we can become true stewards of our planet and ensure its magnificence for generations to come.

So, my friend, I invite you to continue on this incredible voyage of discovery. Let's dive deeper into the captivating world of the TExES Core Subjects EC-6. It's a journey of enlightenment and fulfillment, where we'll conquer the seas of knowledge and reach new heights of success.

Cultural Diversity and Traditions

Come on, folks! Get ready to dive headfirst into the totally cool world of cultural diversity and traditions. With each step we take, we're embarking on an epic journey that's gonna take us all around the globe, through mind-blowing customs, and right into the hearts and minds of diverse communities. This chapter is gonna blow your mind, trust me.

Alright, let's get into it. We're gonna unravel the rich tapestry of human experiences, digging deep into the customs and practices that define different cultures. Picture this: vibrant colors exploding all over, captivating rhythms that make your heart race, and celebrations that are like a big, juicy piece of the cultural pie. It's gonna be a wild ride!

Our first stop? Africa, baby! Prepare to be blown away by the traditions that have been passed down through generations, becoming an essential part of who these African communities are. We're talking about the rhythmic beats and crazy dances of the Masai tribe in Kenya, and the enchanting Lion Dance of the Ewe people in Togo. These ancient customs breathe life, energy, and the spirit of Africa.

Now, let's move our feet a bit east. Get ready to be mesmerized by the enchanting world that is Asia. Picture this: elaborate dragon boat races in China, graceful moves in Thai classical dance, and the deep spiritual vibe of Diwali, the Festival of Lights, in India. Oh, and we can't forget about taekwondo in Korea. This chapter is gonna take us on a spiritual journey, folks. Trust me, it's gonna be powerful.

Now, buckle up for the whirlwind tour of Europe. Get ready for centuries-old traditions that are still shaping modern societies. We'll get to experience the vibrant festivities of Carnival in Venice, where masks and costumes are the name of the game. And let me tell ya, we're gonna be on the edge of our seats as we delve into the enchanting myths and legends of Irish folklore. Flamenco dances in Spain, Oktoberfest in Germany—tradition brings communities together, guys.

Last but definitely not least, we're headed south—way down to Latin America. Brace yourselves for a cultural explosion of music, dance, and color. We'll be savoring the rhythms and getting our groove on with Salsa in Cuba and Tango in Argentina. And hold onto your hats because we're gonna immerse ourselves in the vibrant celebrations of Day of the Dead in Mexico. We're diving deep into the connection between life and death here, people. It's gonna be intense.

As we continue on this crazy journey and soak in all the customs, celebrations, and traditions from around the world, one thing becomes crystal clear—we're all incredibly different, and that's what makes us so damn special. So let's embrace those differences, folks. Let's appreciate the beautiful tapestry of humanity that we're all a part of. Together, we can create a brighter future for everyone. Come on, join me on this mind-blowing adventure as we celebrate cultural diversity and traditions. Let's open up our hearts and minds and let the magic of customs and celebrations bring us all together.

10

Economics

Economic Systems

When we dive into the world of economic systems, we're not just unraveling some boring old theory. No, we're exploring a tapestry so intricate, it's like navigating a maze of dazzling patterns and colors. And if we want to understand how this tapestry is woven, we need to look at the different threads that shape it.

One of the threads that stands out is how stuff gets made - the mode of production. It's all about how we use land, labor, money, and good ol' entrepreneurial spirit to create the things we need and want. You see, the way we produce stuff affects how efficient and successful a country's economy is.

But there's more to it than that. Another crucial thread is how we decide who gets what. We're talking about the allocation of resources - scarce resources, to be precise - and it's a big deal. It's about figuring out how we divvy up the limited goodies to satisfy our boundless desires. We can let the market do its thing, or we can let the government step in. Heck, we can even mix it up and have a bit of both. But understanding the ins and outs of each method is key to unraveling the mysteries of economic systems.

Now, buckle up, 'cause things are about to get even more interesting. See, economic systems are shaped by how much the government sticks its nose in business. At one end, you've got the hands-off approach, where the government just sits back and lets the market run wild. At the other end, you've got the heavyweights who want to control everything, making all the decisions about what gets produced and who gets what. And then there's everything in-between - the mixed economy, where we try to balance marketplace freedom with a little dose of government oversight.

And wait, there's more! Economic systems also have something to do with property rights. It's like the legal framework of who owns what, who gets to use what, and who can sell what. Having strong property rights is super important 'cause it encourages people to invest, innovate, and grow the economy. Some systems let individuals or businesses own stuff, while others have more of a communal vibe where everyone shares the wealth.

Oh, and we can't forget about economic inequality. Yeah, the distribution of wealth, income, and resources - it's a big deal. Some systems work hard to make things more equal, reducing the gaps between the haves and have-nots. Whereas others kinda let individuals fend for themselves, and that means you'll see some serious differences in what people have.

Now, you might be thinking, "Why do I need to know all this? Is it just for those fancy economist folks?" Nah, friend, it's way more than that. Understanding economic systems is like having a superpower. It helps us make sense of how things work in our crazy interconnected world. It shows us why some countries have loads of stuff and others always seem to be falling short.

And lucky for you, Test Treasure Publication gets it. We know just how important it is to wrap your head around all this economic system stuff. That's why our study guides are like little treasure maps, leading you through the twists and turns, revealing the secrets of this mind-boggling subject. So come join us, embark on a wild journey of discovery, and let our resources be your guiding light as you unlock the secrets of economic systems and find your own pathway to success.

Personal Finance

Let me take you on a journey back in time, centuries ago when life was all about bartering. Picture this - people trading goods directly for other goods, relying on trust and the sheer necessity of it all. It was a simpler time, when the notion of currency was just getting started.

But then boom, the 19th century hit, and it brought along something revolutionary - the Industrial Revolution. This game-changer turned the world upside down, transforming economies and societies at lightning speed. With industries booming and trade flourishing, the need for financial institutions arose. And just like that, banks became these beacons of stability, offering folks a secure place to deposit their hard-earned cash and earn some sweet interest in return. It was like finding a hidden treasure chest of security and financial growth.

Now, let's fast forward a bit to the early 20th century. This was when the idea of consumer credit burst onto the scene, turning personal finance on its head. Suddenly, people wanted to keep up with the modern world; they craved all the fancy stuff and convenient luxuries. And credit cards and personal loans were there to make it happen. You could buy now and pay later, which sounded pretty appealing. But of course, with that came the responsibility of managing debt and dealing with those pesky interest rates - two sides of the same coin.

Hold onto your seat because the late 20th century brought about a whole new era in personal finance. Globalization and mind-blowing technological advancements changed the game once again. Think about it: electronic transfers, online banking, and digital currencies. Suddenly, we could do everything from the comfort of our own home, away from those long bank lines and paperwork. It was a game-changer, giving us the power to manage our finances with ease no matter where we were.

And that brings us to today, ladies and gents, where financial literacy is the star of the show. People are finally waking up to the importance of understanding and taking control of their finances. We're seeing all these cool programs and initiatives popping up left and right, wanting to educate us on the ins and outs of budgeting, saving, investing, and planning for the future. The goal is simple: to empower us to make smart and informed financial decisions, so we can lead a life filled with security and prosperity.

Now, personal finance is this massive universe full of exciting topics. We're talking budgeting, debt management, investing, retirement planning, and so much more. It's like a swirling, dynamic world that's always changing as society and economies evolve.

But hey, don't worry. As we venture deeper into the realm of personal finance, we'll explore these fundamental concepts together. We'll untangle the complexities, offering you practical strategies for financial success. Are you ready for this enlightening journey? Buckle up, because we're about to unlock the secrets to building wealth, securing our future, and living a life grounded in financial well-being. Let's do this together, my friend.

11

SCIENTIFIC INQUIRY

Scientific Method

Step 1: Question

Alright, so let's kick this whole journey off with a question. It's like a little spark of curiosity that just gets us all amped up to venture into the unknown. I mean, think about it - every cool discovery in science starts with someone being like, "Hey, I wonder how this thing works?" So, dear friend, don't be afraid to ask. Let that question guide you straight to the juicy nuggets of knowledge.

Step 2: Research

Now that you've got your question, it's time to dive headfirst into the sea of knowledge. Seek out the wisdom of the brainiacs who came before us, scour the archives of scientific papers, and dig through all those databases. It's like embarking on a treasure hunt, except instead of gold doubloons, you're looking for nuggets of information. But trust me, when you stumble upon that perfect nugget, it's like uncovering a hidden gem. Your question starts getting clearer, and suddenly the whole subject comes alive.

Step 3: Hypothesis

Alright, buckle up, 'cause now it's time to let our imagination run wild. Based on all the knowledge we've gathered, it's time to craft our very own hypothesis - our bold statement that challenges what we know about reality. This is where we get to be daring dreamers, pushing the boundaries of what's possible. So, go ahead and throw caution to the wind. After all, it's when we think big that innovation happens.

Step 4: Experimentation

Now things start getting real. It's time to roll up those sleeves and dive headfirst into some good old-fashioned experimentation. Grab your lab coat, fetch your test tubes, and light up those Bunsen burners. It's like being in a mad scientist's lair, but in a totally awesome way. This is where we put our hypothesis to the ultimate test. We observe every tiny little thing, 'cause you never know when that one little detail might just blow your mind and reveal the secrets hidden under our noses.

Step 5: Analysis

Alright, time to geek out on some serious data. Bring out your findings and let's start dissecting them. Look for patterns, connections, and all those little details that make this whole thing come alive. And hey, don't forget to embrace the power of math and logic. They're like the sidekicks that help us unravel the story hidden within our results. So be meticulous, my fellow data enthusiast, 'cause that's where the juiciest revelations often hide.

Step 6: Conclusion

Now that we've analyzed the heck out of our data, it's time to bring it all together and draw some solid conclusions. Take a good long look at the evidence, weigh the pros and cons, and really think about what it all means. And hey, don't forget to think big! Consider the impact that your discoveries might have on the scientific community and the world. It's your chance to be the storyteller of your scientific journey.

Step 7: Communication

Last but definitely not least, it's time to share your discoveries with the world. And trust me, you have a voice that deserves to be heard. Whether it's through scientific papers, conferences, or just good ol' public forums, let your story shine. Become a master storyteller, captivating your audience with the tale of your scientific adventure. Who knows, maybe you'll even inspire someone else to embark on their own journey of discovery. 'Cause hey, knowledge is meant to be shared.

And there you have it, my dear reader. A step-by-step guide to the incredible dance we call the Scientific Method. Use it as your guiding star as you navigate the wild world of science. Embrace its beauty, its rigor, and its power to shape the future. 'Cause who knows what amazing discoveries are waiting for those brave enough to embark on this extraordinary journey.

Data Analysis and Interpretation

Let me tell you about the fascinating world of data analysis. It's like a beautiful dance between art and science, where technical skills and critical thinking perform a delicate balancing act. We dive into a wide range of methods and techniques, transforming raw data into something meaningful and actionable. It's like we're unlocking the hidden potential of information, painting a vivid picture of knowledge.

Our journey begins by understanding the sheer importance of data in decision-making. It's the backbone of everything we do, shaping our conclusions and strategies. Data analysis takes this raw material and turns it into sparkling insights, allowing us to make informed choices that lead to success. Imagine having this superpower of transforming information into wisdom.

To make sense of the chaos of data, we delve into the art of organization and cleaning. It's like untangling a messy ball of yarn. We explore different strategies to collect, categorize, and structure the data, making sure everything is accurate and coherent. This is the foundation for our analysis, setting the stage for those "ah-ha" moments when we uncover hidden treasures.

As we journey further into the world of data analysis, we encounter a whole spectrum of statistical techniques and methodologies. It's like discovering a hidden underground city with its own unique culture and language. Descriptive statistics give us a neat summary of the data, while inferential statistics take us deeper, allowing us to draw conclusions about the whole population from just a sample. Each method is like a puzzle piece that reveals the underlying patterns and relationships within the data.

But we don't just stop at numbers and tables. We bring the data to life through visualization. It's like painting with colors and shapes, bringing emotions and stories to the surface. Graphs, charts, and diagrams become our trusty sidekicks, helping us spot patterns, anomalies, and communicate our findings with impact. These visuals push us to uncover those hidden gems buried beneath the surface.

Finally, we reach the pinnacle of our journey: data interpretation. It's like stepping into a magical realm where the data whispers its secrets, and we become wizards of knowledge. Armed with our analytical skills and critical thinking, we dive deep into the stories that data tells, shaping our understanding of the world. It's like solving a thrilling mystery, revealing the truth and making connections that others may have missed.

Throughout our adventure, we don't just sit back and listen. We roll up our sleeves and dive into hands-on exercises and practical examples. We want to make this knowledge tangible, to feel the thrill of solving real-world problems and making informed decisions. We bridge theory with reality, embracing the power of practicality.

And as we come to the end of this chapter, we emerge with a newfound appreciation for the power of data analysis and interpretation. We've cracked the code and turned numbers into wisdom. Equipped with these skills, we are ready to face the challenges of a data-driven world, where insights are the currency of success. So let's go out there and conquer the data universe!

12

Life Science

Biological Concepts

Let start this journey by delving into the hidden secrets of cell biology. We're diving beneath the surface to uncover the intricate machinery that keeps all living things up and running. Picture it like an architect crafting an awe-inspiring structure. Cells are the master builders, constructing, synthesizing, and regulating to bring life's blueprint to fruition. It's like a whole universe nestled within these tiny organelles that work together to keep everything ticking. From the powerhouse efficiency of mitochondria to the mind-bending maze of the endoplasmic reticulum, we're peeling back the layers to reveal the wonders of these molecular factories.

And as our sights widen, we stumble upon the mind-blowing world of genetics. Brace yourself! We're uncovering the enigma locked within our DNA. It's like unearthing the sacred code that defines every unique trait and characteristic we possess. Weaves of the double helix unfold before our eyes, revealing the captivating elegance of base pairing and the elaborate dance of transcription and translation. Every little step exposes the extraordinary mechanisms that weave life's tapestry, from inheritance and genetic variation to the role of pesky mutations in evolution.

But we're not stopping there, my friend! Say hello to the incredible diversity of life. Get ready to dive deep into the murky world of classification and taxonomy. We're like explorers trekking through the branches of the tree of life, unveiling the hidden relationships between species, families, and kingdoms. From those curious little prokaryotes to the more complex eukaryotes, from bacteria to fungi, we're simply in awe of Mother Nature's brilliance. Each organism is a masterpiece on its own, unraveling the secrets of evolution and adaptation that have shaped our world.

Hold on tight as we venture further into the inner workings of living things, my pal. Get ready to witness the intricate dance of homeostasis and body system regulation. It's like a delicate tightrope walk for the endocrine system, while the circulatory, respiratory, and digestive systems work together in perfect harmony. Everything is a symphony of life in action. Brace yourself, because we're about to unlock the mysteries of cellular respiration, photosynthesis, and the marvelous cycling of matter. We're connecting the dots, bridging the gap between the smallest processes and the grand patterns of ecology.

In this chapter, we're not just skimming the surface of Biological Concepts. Oh no, we're diving headfirst into the deep end, embracing the awe-inspiring beauty and mind-boggling complexity that defines life itself. Every turn of the page unveils the mysteries of cells, genes, and organisms, revealing the profound truths that intertwine us with the graceful elegance of life. So come on, let's embark on this adventure together and uncover the wonders of biology that connect us all.

Ecology and Environmental Science

Let's take a journey through the epic timelines of Ecology and Environmental Science, my friends. Trust me, it's a wild ride. We'll go from ancient times when people actually cared about our natural world, all the way to today's efforts to fix the mess we've made. Hang on tight, 'cause this field has seen some mind-blowing evolution.

Okay, so first stop is waaaay back in the past. Picture our ancestors, living in a time before iPhones and fast food. They actually lived in harmony with nature, believe it or not. Ancient folks like the Mesopotamians, Egyptians, and Mayans, they got it. They knew that everything on this Earth is connected – plants, animals, humans, the works. They respected that connection, 'cause they knew their survival relied on the health of their environment. They were smart, these guys. They practiced sustainable agriculture and even had a spiritual love for nature. And guess what? Their wisdom paved the way for what we know today as ecological principles.

Now, let's fast forward to the 18th and 19th centuries, the time of heroes like Carl Linnaeus and Charles Darwin. These guys completely rocked the scientific world. Linnaeus came up with a system to classify living organisms, like the ultimate organizer. And Darwin? Oh boy, he blew our minds with his theory of natural selection. He showed us how species evolved and diversified over time. Their work not only set the foundation for modern ecology, but also fueled a burning curiosity in scientists to delve deeper into the secrets of nature.

Jump ahead to the 20th century, my friends. Things were heating up – and not just the temperature. People were getting worried about the damage caused by all that industrialization and pollution. But fear not, 'cause environmental pioneers like Rachel Carson stepped up to the plate. Carson wrote a book called "Silent Spring" that exposed how harmful pesticides were messing up our environment. Her work woke up the world and made everyone realize we needed to protect our precious resources, like, ASAP. Cue the establishment of environmental laws and organizations dedicated to saving the Earth.

And here we are today, standing on the edge of a pretty scary climate crisis and a whole lot of environmental destruction. That's why the field of Ecology and Environmental Science is more important than ever. Our scientists are pushing the limits, unraveling the incredibly tangled web of relationships between us, other beings, and the Earth. They're studying how climate change is screwing up our biodiversity and coming up with cool ways to manage our resources sustainably. These peeps are basically the superheroes of our time, fighting for a world where humans and nature coexist peacefully.

As I dive deeper into this field, I'm filled with a mix of awe and responsibility. It's a big job, folks. We've gotta be good guardians of this planet. The knowledge we gain from Ecology and Environmental Science empowers us to make smart choices and take action to protect the beauty and integrity of our Earth for future generations. Together, we have the power to build a sustainable future, where all forms of life can thrive in perfect harmony. Let's do this, my friends.

13

PHYSICAL SCIENCE

Properties of Matter

Chapter 1: Understanding Matter

Imagine standing at the edge of a vast ocean, mesmerized by the crashing waves and the infinite horizon that stretches before you. It's as if the ocean holds the secrets of the universe, just waiting to be unraveled. In our exploration of matter, we too embark on a journey, into the very essence of what makes up our world.

Let me pose a thought-provoking question to you: What is matter? It's like trying to grasp the invisible, to hold onto something intangible. But fear not, for together we will delve into the depths of this enigma. We'll start by classifying matter into three states: solid, liquid, and gas.

Picture a solid, like a towering mountain that stands tall and immovable. Its particles are tightly packed, clinging onto each other with a strength that seems unbreakable. Now visualize a liquid, like a flowing river that meanders through the land. Its molecules slide past one another, finding freedom in their dance. And finally, imagine a gas, like a gentle breeze that moves invisibly across the sky. Its atoms roam freely, without any sense of confinement.

Each state of matter has its own set of properties, like unique fingerprints that set them apart. Solids, with their firm structure, can be shaped and formed into magnificent creations. Liquids, with their adaptability, can take the shape of any container they're poured into. And gases, with their freedom, can fill any space they are given.

Now, close your eyes and picture a block of ice melting under the warmth of the sun. Can you feel the anticipation building? The solid melting into a liquid, water droplets forming and flowing like tiny rivers. It's a transformation that shows us how matter can change, adapting and shifting with the conditions it's exposed to.

Chapter 2: Physical Properties of Matter

Welcome to Chapter 2, where we dive deeper into the physical properties that define matter. We're peeling back the layers, revealing the unique characteristics that make each substance one-of-a-kind.

Think about holding a feather delicately in your palm. It's weightless, barely making a dent on your senses. That's mass, a measure of how much matter an object contains. And as we explore volume, imagine pouring water into a glass, watching it rise and fill every nook and cranny. Volume is the measure of how much space an object occupies.

But let's not stop there. Density is like a magician's trick, revealing the relationship between mass and volume. It's the secret formula that tells us if something will float or sink. And without temperature, our world would be static, frozen in time. It's the invisible force that affects matter's behavior, making it expand or contract, rise or fall.

These properties, intertwined like threads in a tapestry, impact each other in ways we can't always anticipate. A change in temperature can cause a substance to change its state, like water turning into steam when it boils. It's a dance of interconnectedness, where one property waltzes with another.

Chapter 3: Chemical Properties of Matter

Now, let's venture into the captivating world of chemical properties. It's like peering through a kaleidoscope, where the colors shift and blend, revealing hidden potentials and transformative powers.

Think about a matchstick, poised to ignite. When lit, it glows with a fiery passion, igniting a chain reaction. That's a chemical reaction, where one substance transforms into another, releasing energy in the process. It's like watching a caterpillar become a butterfly, a metamorphosis that captivates our imagination.

Catalysts, the unsung heroes of the chemical world, propel these reactions forward, speeding up their journey. They're like magical ingredients, the quiet sparks that bring about great change. And as we witness these reactions unfold, we see matter embracing its true nature, unmasking its hidden potential.

Imagine a world without the power of chemical properties. It would be a monotonous existence, devoid of flavor and color. It's the chemical properties that breathe life into our surroundings, shaping the world we inhabit.

Chapter 4: Changes in Matter

In Chapter 4, we embark on a thrilling adventure, exploring the fascinating transformations that matter loves to undergo. It's as if we're witnessing magic unravel before our eyes, as matter morphs and changes its form.

Let's imagine a cube of sugar dissolving in a cup of hot coffee. Can you feel the suspense building within you? The sugar particles, once held together by unseen forces, now breaking free in a delicate dance. It's a physical change, a shift from solid to liquid, as the sugar particles mingle with the coffee molecules.

But that's not all. Chemical changes lurk in the shadows, waiting for their moment to shine. It's like watching a phoenix rise from the ashes, a rebirth that transforms matter at its core. We unravel the complexities behind melting, boiling, freezing, and evaporation, each change revealing a different facet of matter's nature.

And let's not forget about energy, the mighty force that shapes the destiny of matter. It's like the conductor of an orchestra, guiding the movements of each instrument. Energy can make matter dance, transforming it into something new, or it can freeze it in time, preserving its essence.

Chapter 5: The Periodic Table

In our final chapter, we turn our attention to the Periodic Table, a treasure trove of elements that make up the tapestry of matter. It's like opening a vault, filled with secrets waiting to be deciphered.

As we unravel the organization of this iconic table, patterns emerge, like constellations in the night sky. Atomic number and atomic mass guide us, leading us along the path of understanding. We decode the language of periods and groups, where elements reveal their connections and similarities.

But the Periodic Table is not just a collection of numbers and symbols. It's a storybook, filled with fascinating anecdotes of discovery and wonder. Memorize it like a song, with mnemonics and tricks that make the elements come alive.

So, get ready to take a deep dive into the world of matter. We're embarking on an extraordinary odyssey, where mysteries will be unraveled and beauty will be embraced. Together, let's unlock the secrets of matter and discover the wonders that shape our physical reality.

Forces and Motion

Step right up, folks! Welcome to the wild world of physics, where the invisible forces that run the show are about to be revealed. Buckle up and get ready to dive into the mesmerizing realm of forces and motion, where we'll be taking a historical tour that shaped our understanding of this mind-bending aspect of the natural world.

First stop: Ancient Greece. Picture this: it's way back in the day, and a legendary philosopher named Aristotle takes center stage. His ideas about motion might seem a bit primitive now, but back then, they were absolute game-changers. According to Aristotle, things moved because they were on a quest to find their happy place in the universe - heavy objects going down and lighter ones floating on up. It was simple yet awe-inspiring, and it paved the way for more curious souls to unravel the secrets of motion.

Fast forward a few centuries, and welcome to the Scientific Revolution of the 17th century. Standing in the spotlight is none other than Sir Isaac Newton, a brilliant mind with a knack for shaking things up. Newton's Three Laws of Motion are the superheroes of classical physics, giving us the tools we need to understand the incredible mechanisms that propel stuff around in space. Thanks to him, we gained some serious clarity about how forces work and learned how to predict the behavior of objects with jaw-dropping precision.

Now sounds from the 19th century start creeping up, and you better believe it's about to get electrifying. James Clerk Maxwell, a true wizard in his own right, made groundbreaking discoveries about electromagnetism that rocked our world. His fancy-schmancy equations brought together electricity and magnetism, allowing us to unleash the power of technology like radio waves and wireless communication. It was like a crazy leap forward in our understanding of the forces and motion that rule our universe. Talk about a real game-changer.

And that wasn't all, my friends. The 20th century? Woah, hold onto your hats, because things are about to get trippy. Enter the world of quantum physics, where big guns like Albert Einstein and Niels Bohr turned everything we thought we knew on its head. They introduced mind-boggling concepts like relativity and quantum mechanics that shattered our old-fashioned ideas about cause and effect. Their work didn't just shift the way we thought about forces and motion — it rocked the very foundation of reality itself. Beat that, Aristotle!

But here we are in the present day, my fellow explorers. Forces and motion are still here to blow our minds. Each new discovery peels back yet another layer of the jaw-dropping complexity and beauty that lies within the forces shaping our universe. From the mind-blowing exploration of gravitational waves to the captivating study of quantum entanglement, we just keep diving deeper and deeper into this captivating branch of physics, constantly evolving our understanding of forces and motion.

So, get ready to join me on this wild ride through the centuries. Let's follow the breadcrumbs of history and unravel the ideas and theories that propelled us forward, shedding light on the invisible forces that hold our world together. Together, we'll delve into the mind-bending concepts, mind-blowing laws, and mind-expanding phenomena that define this captivating field of physics. Get ready to have your mind blown, one page at a time. Let the adventure begin!

Energy and Waves

Hey there! Get ready to dive into the fascinating world of energy and waves. Seriously, these things affect everything around us, even when we can't see it happening. It's mind-blowing!

Alright, let's start with Step 2: Understanding the Nature of Energy. We're gonna dig deep into what makes energy tick. We'll explore the different forms it can take, like the energy we get from moving around, or the energy trapped and waiting to be released in objects. Plus, we'll talk about how it can be transferred and transformed - I'm talking mind-blowing concepts like work, power, and the conservation of energy. Get ready to have your mind blown!

Moving on to Step 3: Exploring Waves. Waves are like these graceful messengers carrying vital information through space and time. We'll unravel the secrets behind how waves behave, from their amplitude and frequency to their wavelength. Sound waves, light waves - we'll explore all kinds of waves and the amazing things they create. Trust me, it's gonna be magical.

Step 4: The Electromagnetic Spectrum. Get ready to journey through a whole spectrum of radiant energy. We'll delve into the invisible realms of X-rays and gamma rays, ooh and aah at the vibrant colors of visible light, and bask in the soothing embrace of infrared and radio waves. And hey, did you know these waves have practical applications in communication, medicine, and technology? Prepare to be amazed!

Now, let's tackle Step 5: Energy Transformations and Conservation. This is where things start to get really interesting. We'll explore how energy and waves are connected, and what happens when they come together. We'll even dig into the generation and distribution of electrical energy. Oh, and keep an eye out for electromagnetic radiation - it's a game-changer. It's gonna blow your mind!

In Step 6, we're taking it to the real world. We'll see how energy and waves are actually used in renewable energy sources and cutting-edge technology. This is where we'll really see how these concepts shape our day-to-day lives. And hey, it's not all rainbows and unicorns - we'll also dive into the environmental and societal impacts that come hand in hand with their use. It's gonna be eye-opening.

Almost done! Step 7 is all about practice and review. We're gonna put our newfound knowledge to the test with a bunch of exercises and comprehensive reviews. We want to make sure we've really got this stuff down pat. Get ready to flex those brain muscles!

Finally, in Step 8, we reflect on our epic journey through the world of energy and waves. We'll take a moment to appreciate everything we've learned and how it's shaped us personally. Armed with this incredible knowledge, we'll say goodbye to this chapter and get ready for what's next on our learning adventure.

So let's keep that symphony of energy and waves resonating within us as we forge ahead, wiser and more empowered than ever before. It's gonna be an amazing ride!

14

EARTH AND SPACE SCIENCE

Earth's Structure and Processes

Chapter 1: The Earth's Layers

Come on, folks! We're about to embark on a wild ride deep into the heart of our planet. Buckle up and hold on tight as we peel back the layers of mystery and uncover the secrets that lie beneath our feet.

Imagine descending into the core of the Earth, where staggering heat and pressure give birth to the force that keeps us going - geothermal energy. It's like the lifeblood of our planet, fueling everything from volcanic activity to the movement of continents. It's a fiery world down there, pulsing and throbbing with power and potential.

But, don't worry, we won't stay too long in the blazing depths. We'll make our way to the mantle, which acts as the guardian of our planet's stability. Picture a sea of molten rock, constantly swirling and flowing like an invisible river. It's the conductor of Earth's symphony, shaping our landscapes over millions of years.

Finally, we'll ascend to the crust, the thin and fragile shell that cradles and supports life as we know it. Think of it as our planet's skin, teeming with all sorts of living creatures and awe-inspiring sights. From towering mountains to serene oceans, the crust is where the action is.

Chapter 2: Plate Tectonics and Continental Drift

Hey there, adventurers! Get ready to strap on your hiking boots and join us on a journey across the ever-shifting jigsaw puzzle pieces that make up our Earth's crust. These powerful players are called tectonic plates, and they're constantly on the move.

We'll follow in the footsteps of the legendary Alfred Wegener, who had the audacity to propose the mind-boggling idea of continental drift. Imagine continents traveling vast distances, like migrating birds searching for new homes. It's mind-blowing, right?

And let's not forget about the convection currents, those invisible forces beneath our feet. They act like the mighty wind, pushing and pulling the plates, causing them to collide, separate, and crash against each other. It's a dance of pure power and raw beauty, with each step rearranging the Earth's face.

With every quake and tremor, nature reminds us just how small we are. But it's also a reminder of the grandeur and mightiness of the forces that shape our world. Majestic mountains, deep trenches, and volcanoes rising from the ground - they're all evidence of this ongoing tango of tectonic plates.

Chapter 3: Volcanoes and Earthquakes

Step right up, folks! This chapter is not for the faint-hearted. Brace yourselves as we dive headfirst into the realm of fiery creation and bone-rattling destruction. We're talking about the domain of volcanoes and earthquakes.

Picture yourself standing on the edge of a volcano, gazing down into the gaping mouth of molten rock. It's a sight that both mesmerizes and terrifies, as the Earth gives birth to new land amidst chaos and explosions. And what's left behind? Soil so rich and fertile that it's practically begging for life to take root and flourish.

But earthquakes, oh boy. They're like the Earth's way of throwing a tantrum, reminding us of its power and unpredictability. We'll walk in the footsteps of seismologists, those brave souls who decipher the subtle whispers of the Earth's rumblings. It's a constant reminder that beneath our feet lies a force that can shape our world in an instant.

Feel that rumble? It's the untamed power that keeps us on our toes, forever reshaping the landscapes around us. Just remember to hold on tight and appreciate the beauty that arises from such chaos.

Chapter 4: Weathering and Erosion

Now, my friends, we're entering a realm where the elements themselves become artists, sculpting and polishing the face of our planet. Welcome to the captivating world of weathering and erosion.

Picture the relentless dance of wind, water, ice, and gravity - the ultimate creators of beauty. Waterfalls cascading down majestic cliffs, carving out grand canyons and leaving behind intricate arches and caves. It's a spectacle that showcases the delicate balance between strength and fragility.

There are different types of weathering and erosion at play here. Some are like gentle caresses, slowly wearing away at rocks over time. Others are like fierce hurricanes, tearing through mountains and leaving behind nothing but rubble. It's an ever-changing dance that paints the landscape in different shades and hues.

The Earth is like a canvas, and these natural forces are the brushes that create a tapestry of breathtaking beauty. From towering cliffs to serene valleys, there's no denying the transformative power of weathering and erosion.

Chapter 5: Earth's Resources and Sustainability

Ah, my fellow adventurers, we've reached the final chapter of our journey. It's time to confront the delicate balance between exploitation and preservation, the realm of Earth's resources and sustainability. It's a sobering topic, but one that we must face head-on.

Our Earth holds a treasure trove of resources, from gleaming metals to precious fossil fuels. They're like gifts from the depths, waiting to be discovered and utilized. But they come with a price. We have a responsibility - to ourselves and future generations - to use these resources wisely, without depleting them entirely.

We walk a tightrope between progress and preservation, knowing that our actions today affect the world of tomorrow. It's a daunting task, but with awareness and determination, we can strive for sustainable practices and ensure the bounties of the Earth are enjoyed for generations to come.

So, fellow explorers, join us on this awe-inspiring journey. Let's unlock the hidden wonders of our planet and remind ourselves of the interconnectedness of all life. Together, we can make a difference and embark on a path towards extraordinary learning that transcends the ordinary. Welcome to Test Treasure Publication, where the human spirit meets the boundless wonders of our planet.

Astronomy and Space Exploration

Welcome, my friends, to a journey like no other - a journey that will take us to the heavens above and plunge us into the mysterious depths of celestial science. We are about to unravel the intricate beauty and complexity that dwells within the vast expanse of space.

Our adventure begins with a close encounter with the cosmos itself. Prepare to be amazed as we gaze into the depths of space, witnessing a mesmerizing mosaic of distant galaxies, nebulas, and star clusters that paint the cosmic canvas. I promise you, the descriptions and images I will share with you will leave you breathless, capturing the awe-inspiring dance that unfolds above us each night.

But that's not all, my friends! Our celestial rendezvous continues as we turn our attention towards the Moon - our majestic lunar companion. Join me on a lunar expedition as we explore its craters, valleys, and plains. From ancient impact scars that bear witness to a turbulent past, to the tranquility of its moonlit surface, we shall unlock the secrets of this celestial neighbor and its profound influence on our planet.

As we venture further into the solar system, prepare to be captivated by the wonders that await us. Each planet in our celestial family has a unique and breathtaking story to tell. From the scorching heat of Mercury to the icy depths of Neptune, we will uncover the distinct personalities and characteristics that shape these distant worlds.

But hold on tight, my friends, because our celestial odyssey does not stop there! We are about to push beyond the boundaries of our familiar solar system and immerse ourselves in the realm of exoplanets. Brace yourselves for the unexpected, for here we will encounter worlds that defy our expectations and challenge our understanding of the universe. Together, we will delve into the search for habitable exoplanets, shedding light on the possibility of life beyond our own humble planet.

Now, my fellow cosmic travelers, no exploration of astronomy and space would be complete without a discussion of the incredible tools and technologies that enable us to peer into the depths of the universe. Prepare to be dazzled as we journey into the realm of telescopes - both those that rest upon the Earth and those that drift amongst the stars themselves. We shall uncover the advancements in observatory science that have revolutionized our understanding of the vast cosmos.

But let us not forget, my friends, that as we navigate the mysteries of astronomy and space exploration, we must also confront the profound existential questions that arise from within us. Who are we in this vast universe? Are we truly alone? How do we even begin to fathom the immensity of space and our own insignificance within it? These philosophical quandaries challenge us to reflect on our origins and our future in the grand tapestry of existence.

So, my dear companions, with every turn of the page, we shall dive deeper into the enthralling world of astronomy and space exploration. Through vibrant descriptions, captivating narratives, and thought-provoking insights, we shall uncover the dazzling marvels that lie beyond our earthly realm. Our purpose is not merely to arm you with knowledge, but to spark that sense of wonder and curiosity that will accompany you on your own personal odyssey through the cosmos.

So, I ask you, my dear friends, will you join me on this extraordinary journey? Let us embark together on this glorious adventure through the realms of astronomy and space exploration, where the boundaries of the known universe beckon us to discover and the stars themselves become our guiding lights.

15

Fine Arts

Visual Arts

Step 1: Let's Talk about Visual Arts

Alright, folks, let's dive into the world of visual arts. We're talking about painting, drawing, sculpture, photography - you name it, visual arts cover it all. And let me tell you, it's not just about pretty pictures or fancy shapes. These artworks have the power to stir up emotions, challenge our perspectives, and get people talking. They can even break through language barriers and speak right to your very soul.

Step 2: Getting to Know the Basics

Now, to really appreciate and create visual art, you gotta understand the building blocks that make it all happen. We're talking about the elements of art - things like lines, shapes, colors, forms, and textures. These are the essentials that artists use to put together their masterpieces. And as if that wasn't enough, they've got all these design principles to guide 'em too. Think balance, unity, contrast, emphasis, rhythm, and proportion. It's like a recipe for artistic success.

Step 3: Unleashing Creativity in the Classroom

So, here's the dealio, teachers - it's our job to nurture those creative minds in our classrooms. Visual arts are all about self-expression and showing off who you really are. So, we've gotta come up with some fun and hands-on activities to let our students unleash their inner artists. We're talking painting, sculpture-making, collage, and even printmaking. Each one of these artistic adventures is like a doorway to a whole new world of possibilities.

Step 4: Let's Appreciate Some Art

Alright, now we're getting into the good stuff. We want you to really get into the nitty-gritty of art appreciation. There's a whole tapestry of visual arts out there that have shaped our world, and it's time to dive in. Think Impressionism, Cubism, Surrealism, and Abstract Expressionism. These are just a few of the artistic movements that have defined different eras. And don't forget about the amazing artists like Leonardo da Vinci, Frida Kahlo, Vincent van Gogh, and Georgia O'Keeffe. Their creations are like a burst of inspiration, guiding us on our own artistic journey.

Step 5: Art Meets Everything

Now, visual arts don't play by the rules of one subject – they can connect with just about anything. Imagine incorporating art into English, science, math, social studies, or even music. We're talking about creating visual representations of historical events or illustrating scientific concepts. How about designing math patterns that are visually stunning? It's all about breaking down those disciplinary boundaries and deepening students' understanding of the world around them.

Step 6: Celebrating Diversity and Inclusion

Hey, teachers, we've got a mission here - to celebrate the incredible diversity found within the world of visual arts. You see, there's a whole tapestry of cultural expressions waiting to be explored. Let's showcase art from various cultures, ethnicities, and perspectives. African masks, Chinese calligraphy, Aboriginal dot paintings, Mexican muralism - just a few examples of the incredible diversity out there. This exposure helps our students appreciate the uniqueness of every culture, fostering empathy and understanding.

Step 7: Let the Critics Speak

Last but certainly not least, we want our students to become art critics. Yep, you heard that right - they've got opinions, and they deserve to express them. By getting them to analyze artworks, interpret the artist's message, and engage in respectful discussions, we're helping them develop their critical thinking skills and find their own artistic voice. It's all about empowering these budding critics and giving them a sense of agency and intellectual growth.

The world of visual arts is waiting for you, my friends. So as you dive into the TExES Core Subjects EC-6 (391) Study Guide, let's together embrace the transformative power of visual arts. Let's inspire creativity, unlock hidden potential, and ignite that passion for artistic expression within each and every one of our students.

Performing Arts

Step 1: Theater, where the magic happens. Where stories come alive right before our eyes. It's like diving headfirst into a mesmerizing world of imagination. In this chapter, we're gonna break it all down, from how plays are written to the mind-blowing wizardry of stage design. We'll go deep into the different types of theater, from tragic tales to knee-slapping comedies and all the juicy stuff in between. By studying the techniques used by the great playwrights of yesteryear, we'll understand just how powerful storytelling can be and how it moves us to our core.

Step 2: Get ready to get your groove on with dance. We're going on a wild journey full of grace, beauty, and emotion. From ballet to the cutting-edge moves of contemporary dance, we're gonna learn the language of movement. We'll uncover the secrets of choreography, how to move your body in just the right way, and how to make those feelings shine through. We'll also dive into the history and evolution of dance as an art form, and see how it's shaped our culture and rocked our personal world.

Step 3: Can you hear that sweet sound? That's the melody of music tickling your eardrums. Get ready to be transported to a world where harmony reigns supreme. We're gonna unravel the mysterious world of musical theory, explore the different genres that make music so rich, and see how it fits into different cultures. From classical tunes that make your heart soar to the modern beats that make you groove, we'll take a trip through the ages and shine a light on the genius composers and musicians who've given us so much. And once we understand the rhythm, melody, harmony, and timbre, we'll be able to appreciate and even create music that speaks to our souls.

Step 4: Welcome to the mind-blowing world where all the performing arts collide. Theater, dance, and music come together to create something truly magical. It's like the best kind of mash-up where all the artists bring their A-game. We'll explore how each art form enhances and feeds off each other, like ingredients in a recipe for greatness. We'll also see how interdisciplinary collaborations can take us to places we never even dreamed of. Get ready to be blown away by performances that will leave you spellbound.

As we travel through this captivating world, we need to remember the power of creativity, the joy of expressing ourselves, and the way the arts connect us all as humans. So, welcome to the incredible universe of the performing arts. It's a place where anything can happen, where the stage is set for extraordinary moments of pure awesomeness. Let's light that fire inside and embark on this incredible journey through the performing arts together.

Art Appreciation

Step 1: Developing a Aesthetic Sensibility

So, you wanna get in touch with your artsy side, huh? Well, it all starts with cultivating a sharp sense of aesthetics. You know, training your senses to pick up on all the fancy color palettes, textures, shapes, and forms that artists expertly throw into their creations. Lucky for you, our trusty study guide is here to be your compass on this sensory adventure. Get ready to decode the language of art, my friend.

Step 2: Unveiling the Stories Within

Art ain't just a feast for the eyes, my friend. It's like a top-secret treasure chest packed with deep stories and emotions. And in this step, we're gonna crack open that chest and discover all the hidden gems. Our guide is gonna take you on a wild trip through art history, shedding light on the contexts, themes, and symbolism hiding in those famous masterpieces. Prepare to have your mind blown.

Step 3: Expanding Horizons

Guess what? Art doesn't care about borders or time zones. It's everywhere, man. So, in this step, we're gonna celebrate the sheer awesomeness and diversity of artistic expression from around the world. From jaw-dropping frescoes of the Italian Renaissance to the vibrant colors of African tribal art, our study materials will hook you up with a smorgasbord of artistic traditions. Say goodbye to limited perspectives, and say hello to a whole new world of art.

Step 4: Interpreting Artistic Intent

Alright, time to dig deeper, my friend. Art doesn't just talk on the surface level. It's got layers, like an onion. And in this step, we're gonna peel 'em back and figure out what the heck artists are tryna say. Our study materials will introduce you to all the theories and methods of art interpretation. So grab your detective hat and get ready to unlock the secrets hidden within paintings, sculptures, and crazy installations.

Step 5: Engaging in Critique

If you really wanna appreciate art, you gotta get in on the conversation, my friend. It's like having a deep chat with the artwork and the artist. And in this final step, we're inviting you to join the cool kids' club. Polish up your critical thinking skills, find your unique voice as an art critic, and jump right into the discussion. Our study materials will have you doin' interactive exercises and mind-boggling discussions to explore your own take on art. See you on the other side, my friend.

As you dive into the mind-blowing world of art appreciation with our TExES Core Subjects EC-6 (391) Study Guide 2024–2025, be ready to get hooked, my friend. From the stroke of a paintbrush on canvas to the intricate details carved into stone, every piece of art holds a story. So come on, don't be shy. We, at Test Treasure Publication, invite you to break open the mysteries of art and discover the awe-inspiring beauty that's waiting for you. Trust me, you won't regret it.

16

HEALTH AND WELLNESS

Personal Health

Okay, so listen up. If we want to chase after personal health, we gotta really grasp what it's all about. It's way more than just physical well-being, my friend. It's about this whole package deal called holistic health. It's like bringing together the physical, mental, and emotional sides of our lives and finding that sweet spot of balance and vitality, you know?

But here's the thing, personal health is a real tricky thing. It's always changing and influenced by all sorts of factors. It's like this delicate tightrope act that demands constant attention and proactive steps to keep everything in check. We gotta treat our personal health like the priceless treasure it is and give it the care and love it deserves.

So, step two on this wild journey is to assess our personal health situation. This means we gotta do some soul-searching, my friend. We gotta dig deep and take a good hard look at ourselves. It's about being brutally honest and facing both our strengths and weaknesses head-on.

When it comes to assessing, we start with the physical stuff. Are we moving our bodies enough? Are we eating right? How's the sleep game? All these questions help us figure out where we're at and what we need to work on.

But it's not just about the physical, my friend. We also gotta check out our mental and emotional well-being. How are we dealing with stress? Are we taking care of our minds? Do we reach out for help when we need it? These aspects are crucial for our overall health and happiness.

Alright, now it's time for step three: setting some personal health goals. We gotta make 'em SMART, you know? Specific, measurable, attainable, relevant, and time-bound. It's like having a roadmap for our journey towards wellness.

When it comes to goals, we gotta think short-term and long-term. The short-term ones give us those little victories along the way and keep us motivated. The long-term ones help us see the big picture and guide us towards our ultimate vision of health.

But here's the deal, my friend. Goals are pointless if we don't break them down into small steps. We gotta take things one action at a time. Whether it's adding exercise to our routine, eating mindfully, or seeking therapy, every little step counts on this personal health adventure.

Now, it's time to make some lifestyle changes. We gotta shake things up, my friend. From our daily routines to our habits and mindset, it all needs an upgrade. We gotta cultivate some healthy habits, like exercising regularly, eating nutritious food, and making sure we rest and rejuvenate. We gotta nourish our minds through activities that bring us joy and peace. And hey, healthy relationships, asking for support when we need it, and showing ourselves some love and kindness are all part of the package too.

Last but not least, we gotta track our progress and be adaptable. We can't just set goals and forget about 'em, my friend. We gotta keep tabs on our accomplishments, setbacks, and everything in between. Tracking helps us make smart choices and adjust our plans along the way. We can use journals, apps, or even talk to professionals for extra guidance.

So, there you have it, my friend. This step-by-step guide has given you the foundation for an epic journey towards personal health. It's all about understanding, assessing, goal-setting, making changes, and being flexible. This is your chance to take care of that precious treasure called personal health. Remember, it's a lifelong adventure, and with every step you take, you're opening yourself up to a future full of vitality, balance, and incredible possibilities.

Nutrition and Physical Activity

Nutrition and physical activity, my friends, are absolutely crucial for a healthy lifestyle. I mean, they're like two peas in a pod, always hanging out together. Now, when I talk about proper nutrition, I'm talking about eating a balanced diet full of all the good stuff – you know, the essential nutrients, vitamins, and minerals that our bodies need to grow and develop. And when it comes to physical activity, we're talking about any kind of movement that gets those muscles working and burns up energy.

And guys, let me tell you, when you combine these two things, it's like magic. Seriously, they build a strong foundation for your overall well-being and vitality. You feel alive, energized, and ready to take on the world.

But here's the thing, my fellow educators, we've got to understand just how important nutrition and physical activity are for our students' success in school. I'm talking sharper minds, better focus, and improved concentration. And that's not all – these healthy habits can do wonders for a student's mental health too. They boost self-esteem, foster discipline and determination, and help our young learners become the best versions of themselves.

So, when it comes to passing that TExES Core Subjects EC-6 exam, it's not just about knowing your stuff. It's about knowing how to spot and meet the needs of your students. And that means being clued up on nutrition and physical activity.

When you incorporate this knowledge into your teaching practices, you empower your students, my friends. You give them the tools they need to make smart choices about what they eat and how they move their bodies, all in the name of their well-being.

And here's the best part – the fact that the TExES exam includes this topic is a big deal. It shows that they understand just how crucial nutrition and physical activity are in shaping the academic journey of our little learners. So guys, it's time for us educators to step up. We need to arm ourselves with the knowledge and strategies to promote healthy habits in and out of the classroom. Our students are counting on us.

Now, in the chapters ahead, we're going to dive deep into the world of nutrition and physical activity. We're going to unravel all those fancy concepts, like macronutrients and micronutrients. And hey, we're going to learn about the importance of meal planning and understanding those wacky food labels. Oh, and let's not forget all the awesome ways we can encourage our students to get moving.

I've got some seriously cool study guides, engaging activities, and thought-provoking exercises lined up for you. It's going to be a transformative journey, my friends. I'm going to empower you, as an educator, to guide your students towards a future that's full of life, happiness, and success.

So come on, join me. Let's dive headfirst into the world of nutrition and physical activity. Together, we're going to unlock the secrets to unleashing the full potential of our students' academic endeavors. We'll explore the beautiful connection between nourishment and movement and discover all the amazing treasures they hold for the minds and bodies of our future generation. Let's do this!

17

PHYSICAL EDUCATION

Physical Fitness and Exercise

Physical fitness and exercise, my friend, they're not just some passing fad or trend. Nah, they're the very foundation of a good, healthy life. They're the things that make your body strong, your mind sharp, and your spirits soar. Trust me, when you make exercise a part of your regular routine, good things happen.

Now, lemme tell ya, having a balanced exercise routine is key. And that's what we're gonna dig into in this study guide. We gonna cover all the different aspects of fitness, so you can make sure you're hittin' all the right notes. We talkin' strength training, cardio exercises, flexibility exercises, and endurance training. 'Cause, hey, you want the best results, right?

Let's start with strength training. This is where you build up them muscles, my friend. Whether you're pumpin' iron or doin' bodyweight exercises, the goal here is to make yourself look good and feel even better. As you work those muscles, they get stronger, and that means you can handle anything life throws at you without breakin' a sweat.

But hold on, 'cause we can't forget about cardio. This is what gets your heart pumpin' and your lungs singin'. Running, biking, swimming, even bustin' a move on the dance floor, anythin' that gets that heart rate up goes in this category. Not only does it make your heart and lungs work better, but it releases these little feel-good hormones called endorphins, and trust me, that's gonna put a smile on your face.

Now, I know a lot of people might overlook flexibility exercises, but they're super important. We talkin' yoga, Pilates, and stretchin', my friend. These exercises keep your joints movin' smoothly and make sure you don't pull anything. Plus, they help you move more gracefully and keep your body in balance. It's like a dance between strength and flexibility, my friend.

Lastly, we gotta talk about endurance training. Think long-distance running or bikin'. This is where you really push yourself to the limit, both physically and mentally. It's a test of your stamina and your willpower. And let me tell ya, when you push through that wall and keep on goin', you become a true force to be reckoned with.

Now, here's the thing. What works for me might not work for you, and vice versa. That's why it's so important to find your own balance. That's what this study guide is all about, my friend. It's gonna give you all the knowledge you need to tailor your exercise routine to fit your own unique needs and goals.

As you dive into these chapters, you gonna learn about exercise programs, how to stay safe, proper form and technique, and even nutrition. It's all part of the bigger picture, my friend. And armed with this knowledge, you gonna break down all them barriers that have been holdin' you back. You gonna take charge of your body and unleash its full potential. Ain't that somethin'?

Physical fitness and exercise, my friend, they're more than just something you do. They're like lifelong buddies that keep you vital and strong. So, let's take this journey together, my friend, deep into the world of fitness and exercise. With every turn of the page, we gonna uncover a treasure trove of wisdom and ignite that fire inside you. Get ready for a healthier, more fulfilling life, my friend. It's about to get real good.

Sports and Games

Let's talk about sports and games, my friend. They're not just all about the heart-pounding excitement of a basketball game or the elegant twirls of a figure skater. No, they're so much more than that. Sports and games are a testament to the human spirit. They show off our competitive nature and our ability to grow and achieve great things. It's inspiring, really.

And the benefits of sports and games go way beyond the thrill of winning. They make us stronger, both in body and mind. They teach us discipline, focus, and strategic thinking. The lessons we learn on the field or court stick with us and help us overcome the challenges we face in life. Sports give us that resilience and determination to keep pushing forward no matter what.

But you know what's really amazing? It's how sports and games bring people together. They break down all barriers and create connections. It doesn't matter what language you speak or where you come from, sports unite us all. From a little soccer match that lights up a neighborhood to huge international events that unite whole nations, the power of sports to foster camaraderie is simply remarkable.

In this chapter, we're gonna dive deep into the world of sports and games. We'll explore all kinds of disciplines, from team sports like soccer and basketball to individual pursuits like tennis and swimming. I wanna give you a real understanding of each sport, from the technical aspects to the strategies used, and even the physical and mental strength it takes.

But it's not just about winning and losing, my friend. No, sports are about the lessons we learn, the character we build, and the friendships we make along the way. In this book, you'll find stories of legendary sports figures who embody the values of sportsmanship. They'll be your role models, inspiring you to be the best athlete and educator you can be.

Now, in the next chapters, we're gonna help you master the subjects you need for the TExES Core Subjects EC-6 (391) exam. We'll cover everything from English language arts to math, science, and social studies. But hey, our study materials aren't just dry facts and figures. We want to spark your critical thinking, ignite your creativity, and make you fall in love with learning.

Because let me tell you, success is about more than just passing an exam. It's about becoming a lifelong learner and a passionate educator. That's what we're all about here at Test Treasure Publication. We want to empower you with knowledge and tools to make a real impact on your students and the future of education.

So, my friend, are you ready to join us on this enlightening journey? We're gonna explore the world of sports, games, and education and uncover endless possibilities. Together, let's strive for remarkable success, where knowledge, passion, and community come together in perfect harmony. Let's do this!

18.1 FULL-LENGTH PRACTICE TEST 1

English Language Arts and Reading and the Science of Teaching Reading

Question 1: Which of the following strategies is most effective in teaching phonemic awareness to beginning readers?
A) Teaching complex sentence structure
B) Using flashcards with written words
C) Segmenting words into individual phonemes
D) Reading chapter books aloud to students

Question 2: In English grammar, what part of speech modifies a verb, adjective, or another adverb?
A) Noun
B) Adverb
C) Conjunction
D) Pronoun

Question 3: What strategy would best support a student struggling with reading comprehension?
A) Increasing reading speed
B) Providing a summary before reading
C) Memorizing vocabulary words
D) Focusing only on phonics

Question 4: Which phonological awareness skill is most advanced?

A) Rhyming

B) Syllable counting

C) Phoneme isolation

D) Alliteration

Question 5: What is the primary purpose of a text's conclusion?

A) To introduce new ideas

B) To summarize key points

C) To ask questions

D) To provide illustrations

Mathematics

Question 6: If $x=4$ and $y=3$, what is the value of $2x-y$?

A) 5

B) 8

C) 3

D) 9

Question 7: What is the perimeter of a rectangle that has a length of 10 units and a width of 6 units?

A) 32 units

B) 16 units

C) 40 units

D) 30 units

Question 8: What is the next term in the sequence 3,9,27,81,...?

A) 160

B) 243

C) 120
D) 180

Question 9: Which of the following represents a proportional relationship?
A) $y=2x+3$
B) $y=3x$
C) $y=x^2$
D) $y=x/2-1$

Question 10: A car travels 60 miles in 1 hour. How many miles will it travel in 2.5 hours?
A) 120 miles
B) 130 miles
C) 150 miles
D) 140 miles

Social Studies

Question 11: Who was the first President of the United States?
A) Benjamin Franklin
B) Thomas Jefferson
C) George Washington
D) John Adams

Question 12: The Emancipation Proclamation, issued by President Lincoln, had what primary effect?
A) Ended the Civil War
B) Granted women the right to vote
C) Abolished slavery in Confederate states
D) Established the Bill of Rights

Question 13: The Bill of Rights consists of how many amendments to the U.S. Constitution?
A) 5
B) 12
C) 10
D) 15

Question 14: What was the main reason for European exploration and colonization of the Americas during the 15th and 16th centuries?
A) Spreading democracy
B) Seeking religious freedom
C) Finding a cure for diseases
D) Searching for new trade routes and wealth

Question 15: What governmental principle is reflected in the separation of powers among the three branches of government in the U.S.?
A) Federalism
B) Checks and Balances
C) Popular Sovereignty
D) Representative Democracy

Science

Question 16: What is the process by which plants convert sunlight, carbon dioxide, and water into glucose and oxygen?
A) Respiration
B) Fermentation
C) Photosynthesis
D) Digestion

Question 17: What type of rock is formed by the cooling and solidification of lava or magma?

A) Metamorphic

B) Sedimentary

C) Igneous

D) Mineral

Question 18: What is the primary role of the mitochondria in a cell?

A) Protein synthesis

B) Photosynthesis

C) Energy production

D) DNA replication

Question 19: In a food chain, what organism typically comes first?

A) Carnivore

B) Decomposer

C) Producer

D) Consumer

Question 20: Which phase of the water cycle involves water changing from a gas to a liquid?

A) Evaporation

B) Condensation

C) Precipitation

D) Transpiration

Fine Arts, Health, and Physical Education

Question 21: In art, what element is used to create the illusion of depth on a flat surface?

A) Texture

B) Perspective

C) Balance

D) Contrast

Question 22: What vitamin is primarily responsible for healthy bone development and is obtained through sunlight exposure?

A) Vitamin A

B) Vitamin B

C) Vitamin C

D) Vitamin D

Question 23: Which of the following is NOT a component of physical fitness?

A) Flexibility

B) Strength

C) Color coordination

D) Endurance

Question 24: What is the primary purpose of a warm-up before physical exercise?

A) To increase heart rate and blood flow to muscles

B) To immediately achieve peak performance

C) To practice the main activity at full intensity

D) To socialize with others

Question 25: In music, what is the term for a gradual increase in loudness?

A) Crescendo

B) Staccato

C) Forte

D) Allegro

English Language Arts and Reading and the Science of Teaching Reading

Question 26: Which literary device uses exaggeration for emphasis or effect?

A) Irony

B) Metaphor

C) Hyperbole

D) Alliteration

Question 27: What is the main purpose of a thesis statement in an essay?

A) To conclude the argument

B) To summarize each paragraph

C) To introduce the topic and state the author's position

D) To entertain the reader

Question 28: Which of the following is considered a primary source?

A) A biography of Abraham Lincoln

B) A textbook on World War II

C) A letter written by George Washington

D) A documentary on the Civil Rights Movement

Question 29: How do adjectives primarily function in sentences?

A) To link subjects and predicates

B) To describe or modify nouns

C) To show action or state of being

D) To connect independent clauses

Question 30: What type of poetry has a strict 14-line structure and often explores themes of love or philosophy?

A) Limerick

B) Haiku

C) Sonnet

D) Free Verse

Mathematics

Question 31: A cube has a side length of 4 units. What is its volume?

A) 16 cubic units

B) 32 cubic units

C) 48 cubic units

D) 64 cubic units

Question 32: If a shirt is on sale for 20% off and the original price is $50, what is the sale price?

A) $40

B) $30

C) $10

D) $60

Question 33: Which of the following is NOT a prime number?

A) 17

B) 19

C) 21

D) 23

Question 34: What is the slope of the line represented by the equation $y=-3x+6$?

A) 3

B) -3

C) 6

D) 0

Question 35: What is the probability of rolling an even number on a standard six-sided die?

A) 1/3

B) 1/2

C) 1/6

D) 2/3

Social Studies

Question 36: The Marshall Plan was implemented after World War II with the main goal of:

A) Establishing the United Nations

B) Rebuilding European economies

C) Ending the Vietnam War

D) Reducing U.S. military presence abroad

Question 37: The Magna Carta, signed in 1215, was significant for what reason?

A) It abolished slavery in the British Empire

B) It granted women the right to vote

C) It limited the power of the English monarch

D) It established the European Union

Question 38: What economic system emphasizes government control over the means of production and distribution?

A) Capitalism

B) Socialism

C) Feudalism

D) Mercantilism

Question 39: The Emancipation Proclamation issued by Abraham Lincoln in 1863 did what?

A) Ended the Civil War

B) Granted women's suffrage

C) Freed slaves in Confederate-held territory

D) Established the Federal Reserve

Question 40: Which ancient civilization was known for its city-states, such as Athens and Sparta?

A) Egyptian

B) Greek

C) Roman

D) Mesopotamian

Science

Question 41: Which part of the cell is responsible for controlling what enters and exits the cell?

A) Nucleus

B) Mitochondria

C) Ribosomes

D) Cell membrane

Question 42: What is the primary function of the chloroplasts in a plant cell?

A) Cellular respiration

B) Photosynthesis

C) Digestion

D) Reproduction

Question 43: Which type of rock is formed from the cooling and solidification of magma beneath the Earth's surface?

A) Sedimentary

B) Metamorphic

C) Igneous

D) Limestone

Question 44: What type of energy is stored in the bonds of molecules?

A) Kinetic

B) Thermal

C) Chemical

D) Nuclear

Question 45: Which planet is the largest in our solar system?

A) Venus

B) Mars

C) Jupiter

D) Saturn

Fine Arts, Health, and Physical Education

Question 46: What does the term "allegro" indicate in a musical score?

A) Slow tempo

B) Loud volume

C) Fast tempo

D) Soft volume

Question 47: Which artistic movement focused on capturing fleeting moments and the effects of light?

A) Cubism

B) Impressionism

C) Surrealism

D) Romanticism

Question 48: In physical education, what is the primary purpose of a cooldown after exercise?
A) To quickly decrease heart rate
B) To prolong the workout
C) To facilitate recovery and reduce muscle stiffness
D) To increase muscle mass

Question 49: What does a proper diet rich in vitamin C primarily promote?
A) Strong bones
B) Night vision
C) Healthy skin and immune system
D) Weight loss

Question 50: Which of the following dances originated in Brazil?
A) Tango
B) Salsa
C) Samba
D) Waltz

English Language Arts and Reading and the Science of Teaching Reading

Question 51: Which of the following terms describes the narrator's position in relation to the story in a literary text?
A) Theme
B) Tone
C) Point of View
D) Mood

Question 52: Which of the following is an example of onomatopoeia?
A) Crash

B) Like

C) But

D) And

Mathematics

Question 53: If $f(x)=2x^2-3x+4$, what is the value of $f(2)$?

A) 6

B) 10

C) 12

D) 8

Question 54: What is the midpoint of the line segment with endpoints $A(-4,6)$ and $B(4,-2)$?

A) (0, 0)

B) (0, 2)

C) (2, 0)

D) (-2, 0)

Social Studies

Question 55: Who was the first President of the United States?

A) George Washington

B) Thomas Jefferson

C) Benjamin Franklin

D) John Adams

Question 56: What was the main goal of the women's suffrage movement in the early 20th century?

A) Equal pay for women

B) The right to vote for women

C) Ending racial segregation

D) Universal health care

Science

Question 57: Which layer of the Earth's atmosphere contains the ozone layer?

A) Troposphere

B) Stratosphere

C) Mesosphere

D) Thermosphere

Question 58: What is the most common gas in Earth's atmosphere?

A) Oxygen

B) Carbon dioxide

C) Nitrogen

D) Hydrogen

Fine Arts, Health, and Physical Education

Question 59: In ballet, what term is used to describe a full 360-degree turn on one foot?

A) Arabesque

B) Pirouette

C) Plie

D) Tendu

Question 60: What nutrient is primarily responsible for providing energy for body functions?

A) Vitamins

B) Minerals

C) Carbohydrates

D) Proteins

Question 61: In art, what is the term for using different shades of light and dark to create a three-dimensional form?

A) Shading

B) Perspective

C) Contour

D) Hue

Question 62: What is the name of the art movement characterized by an emphasis on expressive, emotional use of paint, often without clear subjects?

A) Abstract Expressionism

B) Realism

C) Pop Art

D) Futurism

Question 63: What is the recommended amount of physical activity for adults per week, according to health guidelines?

A) 30 minutes per day

B) 1 hour per day

C) 150 minutes per week

D) 3 hours per week

Question 64: What is the primary purpose of protein in the diet?

A) Providing energy

B) Building and repairing tissues

C) Aiding in digestion

D) Regulating body temperature

Question 65: In music, what term is used to describe a gradual increase in loudness?

A) Forte

B) Crescendo

C) Allegro

D) Staccato

English Language Arts and Reading and the Science of Teaching Reading

Question 66: What literary device is used when an object or animal is given human characteristics?

A) Simile

B) Metaphor

C) Personification

D) Alliteration

Question 67: In a persuasive essay, what term is used to describe the opposing view to the author's argument?

A) Counterclaim

B) Thesis

C) Claim

D) Summary

Mathematics

Question 68: If $y=3x+7$, what is the slope of the line?

A) 3

B) 7

C) 0

D) -3

Question 69: What is the area of a circle with a radius of 5 units?

A) 25π

B) 10π

C) 5π

D) 50π

Social Studies

Question 70: Which document established the first government of the United States?

A) U.S. Constitution

B) Declaration of Independence

C) Articles of Confederation

D) Bill of Rights

Question 71: What economic system emphasizes individual ownership and a free market?

A) Socialism

B) Communism

C) Capitalism

D) Feudalism

Science

Question 72: What type of rock is formed from the cooling and solidification of lava or magma?

A) Sedimentary

B) Metamorphic

C) Igneous

D) Mineral

Question 73: What is the primary function of the mitochondria in a cell?

A) Photosynthesis

B) Protein synthesis

C) DNA replication

D) Energy production

Fine Arts, Health, and Physical Education

Question 74: What is the art of making objects from clay called?

A) Sculpture

B) Pottery

C) Painting

D) Mosaic

Question 75: Which musical term denotes a gradual decrease in volume?

A) Crescendo

B) Decrescendo

C) Fortissimo

D) Allegro

Question 76: In the context of physical fitness, what does the acronym "FITT" stand for?

A) Frequency, Intensity, Time, Type

B) Fast, Intensity, Training, Tempo

C) Frequency, Interval, Time, Training

D) Fast, Intense, Tempo, Type

Question 77: What type of painting technique involves applying small dots of color to form an image?

A) Impressionism

B) Cubism

C) Pointillism

D) Surrealism

Question 78: What is the main function of fats in the human diet?

A) Building muscles

B) Regulating body temperature

C) Providing energy and storing vitamins

D) Boosting immunity

Question 79: In drama, what term refers to the part of the play where the conflict reaches its highest point?

A) Resolution

B) Exposition

C) Climax

D) Denouement

Question 80: Which of the following is a fundamental principle of modern dance?

A) Strict adherence to classical form

B) Emphasis on storytelling

C) Emphasis on personal expression

D) Focus on traditional narratives

Question 81: What is the process of adding minerals, such as calcium and magnesium, to water called?

A) Filtration

B) Distillation

C) Remineralization

D) Chlorination

Question 82: Which art movement is associated with Salvador Dalí?

A) Impressionism

B) Cubism

C) Surrealism

D) Futurism

Question 83: What type of exercise focuses on the use of controlled movements and breathing to improve flexibility, strength, and balance?

A) Yoga

B) Pilates

C) Aerobics

D) Weightlifting

Question 84: What type of art emphasizes the accurate depiction of life and objects, focusing on real and existing subjects?

A) Abstract

B) Cubism

C) Surrealism

D) Realism

Question 85: What is the recommended method to check for breast cancer at home?

A) X-ray

B) Mammogram

C) Self-examination

D) Blood test

Question 86: Which art technique involves creating images by arranging small colored pieces of glass, stone, or other materials?

A) Sculpture

B) Fresco

C) Mosaic

D) Engraving

Question 87: What nutrient is primarily responsible for strengthening bones and teeth?

A) Iron

B) Vitamin C

C) Protein

D) Calcium

Question 88: What is the term used to describe the emotional quality or mood of a work of art?

A) Composition

B) Hue

C) Texture

D) Tone

Question 89: What is the primary role of carbohydrates in the diet?

A) Building muscles

B) Providing energy

C) Boosting immunity

D) Regulating body temperature

Question 90: In which art movement would you likely find distorted and exaggerated forms to evoke emotion?

A) Baroque

B) Classicism

C) Romanticism

D) Expressionism

English Language Arts and Reading and the Science of Teaching Reading

Question 91: Which of the following is NOT a type of irony?

A) Dramatic Irony

B) Situational Irony

C) Verbal Irony

D) Historical Irony

Mathematics

Question 92: If the lengths of two sides of a right triangle are 6 and 8, what is the length of the hypotenuse?

A) 10

B) 12

C) 14

D) 16

Social Studies

Question 93: Who was the first President of the United States under the Constitution?

A) George Washington

B) Thomas Jefferson

C) John Adams

D) Benjamin Franklin

Science

Question 94: What phase change occurs when a liquid turns into a gas?

A) Condensation

B) Freezing

C) Evaporation

D) Sublimation

Fine Arts, Health, and Physical Education

Question 95: In ballet, what term is used to describe a full 360-degree turn on one foot?

A) Arabesque

B) Pirouette

C) Plie

D) Pas de chat

Question 96: What is the primary benefit of aerobic exercise?

A) Increasing muscle mass

B) Improving cardiovascular health

C) Enhancing flexibility

D) Boosting immunity

Additional Questions from Various Sections

Question 97: What type of poetry consists of five lines with a specific syllable pattern of 5, 7, 5, 7, 7?

A) Sonnet

B) Haiku

C) Limerick

D) Tanka

Question 98: What is the smallest prime number?

A) 0

B) 1

C) 2

D) 3

Question 99: In a democracy, what principle ensures that no single branch of government has unchecked power?

A) Rule of law

B) Separation of powers

C) Social contract

D) Popular sovereignty

Question 100: Which planet is known as the "Red Planet"?

A) Venus

B) Mars

C) Jupiter

D) Saturn

18.2 ANSWER SHEET - PRACTICE TEST 1

1. Answer: C

Explanation: Phonemic awareness refers to the ability to hear and manipulate individual sounds in spoken words. Segmenting words into individual phonemes allows beginners to understand the connection between sounds and letters, which is fundamental to reading.

2. Answer: B

Explanation: Adverbs modify verbs, adjectives, or other adverbs, providing information about how, when, where, why, or to what extent something is done.

3. Answer: B

Explanation: Providing a summary before reading helps students understand the context and main ideas, which can enhance reading comprehension.

4. Answer: C

Explanation: Phoneme isolation, the ability to recognize individual sounds within words, is more advanced than other phonological awareness skills like rhyming, syllable counting, or alliteration.

5. Answer: B

Explanation: The conclusion of a text usually serves to summarize the key points or main ideas, providing closure to the reader.

6. Answer: A

Explanation: Substituting the given values, we have 2x4−3=8−3=5.

7. Answer: A

Explanation: The perimeter of a rectangle is given by 2×length+2×width=2×10+2×6=20+12=32 units.

8. Answer: B

Explanation: This sequence is a geometric progression where each term is multiplied by 3 to get the next term. So, 81×3=243.

9. Answer: B

Explanation: A proportional relationship is represented by a linear equation where the y-intercept is zero. In this case, option B represents a proportional relationship.

10. Answer: C

Explanation: Since the car travels 60 miles in 1 hour, it will travel 60×2.5=150 miles in 2.5 hours.

11. Answer: C

Explanation: George Washington was the first President of the United States, serving from 1789 to 1797.

12. Answer: C

Explanation: The Emancipation Proclamation, issued in 1863, declared that all slaves in Confederate-held territory were to be set free, although it did not end slavery in the entire country.

13. Answer: C

Explanation: The Bill of Rights consists of the first 10 amendments to the U.S. Constitution, outlining fundamental American civil liberties.

14. Answer: D

Explanation: The primary motivation for European exploration and colonization during the 15th and 16th centuries was the search for new trade routes and the acquisition of wealth.

15. Answer: B

Explanation: The separation of powers among the legislative, executive, and judicial branches of government reflects the principle of Checks and Balances, ensuring that no single branch can dominate the others.

16. Answer: C

Explanation: Photosynthesis is the process by which plants use sunlight, carbon dioxide, and water to produce glucose (a sugar) and oxygen.

17. Answer: C

Explanation: Igneous rocks are formed by the cooling and solidification of molten lava or magma.

18. Answer: C

Explanation: The mitochondria, often referred to as the "powerhouse of the cell," are responsible for producing energy in the form of ATP through cellular respiration.

19. Answer: C

Explanation: In a food chain, the producer, such as a plant that uses photosynthesis, typically comes first, providing energy for the rest of the ecosystem.

20. Answer: B

Explanation: Condensation is the phase of the water cycle where water vapor (gas) changes into liquid water, often forming clouds.

21. Answer: B

Explanation: Perspective in art refers to the technique used to represent three-dimensional objects on a two-dimensional surface, creating the illusion of depth.

22. Answer: D

Explanation: Vitamin D is essential for healthy bone development and is synthesized in the skin through exposure to sunlight.

23. Answer: C

Explanation: Color coordination is not a component of physical fitness. Flexibility, strength, and endurance are essential aspects of physical fitness.

24. Answer: A

Explanation: The primary purpose of a warm-up is to gradually increase heart rate and blood flow to the muscles, preparing the body for more strenuous activity.

25. Answer: A

Explanation: A crescendo in music refers to a gradual increase in loudness or intensity, often used to build tension or excitement.

26. Answer: C

Explanation: Hyperbole is a literary device that uses extreme exaggeration to make a point or emphasize an idea.

27. Answer: C

Explanation: The thesis statement introduces the main topic and clearly states the author's position or argument, guiding the direction of the entire essay.

28. Answer: C

Explanation: A primary source is a document or object created by a person directly involved in an event or time period. A letter written by George Washington would be a primary source.

29. Answer: B

Explanation: Adjectives primarily function to describe or modify nouns, giving more detail about characteristics such as size, color, shape, or feelings.

30. Answer: C

Explanation: A sonnet is a 14-line poem with a specific rhyme scheme, often exploring themes such as love or philosophical ideas.

31. Answer: D

Explanation: The volume of a cube is given by the side length cubed, so $4^3=64$ cubic units.

32. Answer: A

Explanation: A 20% discount on a $50 shirt is $10, so the sale price would be $50 - $10 = $40.

33. Answer: C

Explanation: 21 is not a prime number, as it is divisible by 3 and 7. Prime numbers only have two distinct positive divisors: 1 and the number itself.

34. Answer: B

Explanation: In the equation of a line in slope-intercept form, $y=mx+b$, the slope is represented by m. In this case, the slope is -3.

35. Answer: B

Explanation: There are three even numbers on a six-sided die (2, 4, and 6), so the probability of rolling an even number is $3/6=1/2$.

36. Answer: B

Explanation: The Marshall Plan was aimed at rebuilding the war-torn economies of Western Europe after World War II to prevent the spread of communism.

37. Answer: C

Explanation: The Magna Carta was significant because it limited the power of the English monarch, establishing the principle that even the king was subject to the law.

38. Answer: B

Explanation: Socialism emphasizes government control or communal ownership of the means of production and distribution, aiming for wealth and power to be distributed equally among its members.

39. Answer: C

Explanation: The Emancipation Proclamation declared that all slaves in Confederate-held territory were to be set free, although it did not end slavery in the entire nation.

40. Answer: B

Explanation: Ancient Greece was known for its city-states, or polis, such as Athens and Sparta, each with its government and way of life.

41. Answer: D

Explanation: The cell membrane controls what enters and exits the cell, acting as a barrier between the cell's interior and its external environment.

42. Answer: B

Explanation: Chloroplasts in plant cells are responsible for photosynthesis, the process by which plants convert sunlight, carbon dioxide, and water into glucose and oxygen.

43. Answer: C

Explanation: Igneous rocks are formed from the cooling and solidification of magma beneath the Earth's surface or lava on the surface.

44. Answer: C

Explanation: Chemical energy is the energy stored in the bonds of molecules and is released during chemical reactions.

45. Answer: C

Explanation: Jupiter is the largest planet in our solar system, with a diameter of about 86,881 miles (139,822 kilometers). It is a gas giant and has a strong magnetic field.

46. Answer: C

Explanation: "Allegro" is an Italian term used in music to indicate a fast or lively tempo.

47. Answer: B

Explanation: Impressionism was an art movement that focused on capturing fleeting moments, light, and atmosphere, often through loose brushwork and lighter colors.

48. Answer: C

Explanation: The primary purpose of a cooldown after exercise is to facilitate recovery, gradually lower heart rate, and reduce muscle stiffness.

49. Answer: C

Explanation: Vitamin C is essential for the growth, development, and repair of all body tissues. It's involved in many body functions, including the formation of collagen, absorption of iron, the immune system, wound healing, and the maintenance of cartilage, bones, and teeth.

50. Answer: C

Explanation: Samba is a lively, rhythmical dance of Brazilian origin.

51. Answer: C

Explanation: Point of View refers to the narrator's position in relation to the story being told, whether it's a first-person, second-person, or third-person perspective.

52. Answer: A

Explanation: Onomatopoeia is a literary device where a word imitates the natural sound of a thing. "Crash" is an example of onomatopoeia as it represents the sound of something crashing.

53. Answer: A

Explanation: To find $f(2)$, substitute $x=2$ into the equation: $2\cdot(2^2)-3\cdot2+4=2\cdot4-6+4=8-6+4=6$.

54. Answer: B

Explanation: The midpoint of a line segment with endpoints $(x1,y1)$ and $(x2,y2)$ is given by $(x1+x2/2, y1+y2/2)$. So the midpoint of the segment with endpoints $A(-4,6)$ and $B(4,-2)$ is $(-4+4/2, 6-2/2)=(0,2)$.

55. Answer: A

Explanation: George Washington was the first President of the United States, serving from 1789 to 1797.

56. Answer: B

Explanation: The women's suffrage movement in the early 20th century primarily focused on securing the right to vote for women.

57. Answer: B

Explanation: The ozone layer is located within the stratosphere, the second major layer of Earth's atmosphere.

58. Answer: C

Explanation: Nitrogen is the most common gas in Earth's atmosphere, making up about 78% of the air.

59. Answer: B

Explanation: A pirouette is a classical ballet term meaning "spin." It describes a dancer's complete turn of the body on one foot, either on pointe or demi-pointe.

60. Answer: C

Explanation: Carbohydrates are the body's main source of energy, providing the fuel needed for physical activity and proper organ function.

61. Answer: A

Explanation: Shading is the technique of using different shades of light and dark to create the appearance of volume in three-dimensional objects.

62. Answer: A

Explanation: Abstract Expressionism is an art movement characterized by a lack of clear subjects and an emphasis on the expressive, emotional use of paint.

63. Answer: C

Explanation: Health guidelines commonly recommend 150 minutes of moderate-intensity or 75 minutes of vigorous-intensity physical activity per week for adults.

64. Answer: B

Explanation: Protein is essential for building and repairing tissues in the body, such as muscles and organs.

65. Answer: B

Explanation: A crescendo in music refers to a gradual increase in loudness or intensity.

66. Answer: C

Explanation: Personification is the literary device where human characteristics or qualities are attributed to an inanimate object or animal.

67. Answer: A

Explanation: A counterclaim is the opposing view or alternative argument to the author's main claim in a persuasive essay.

68. Answer: A

Explanation: The slope of the line is represented by the coefficient of x in the equation, which in this case is 3.

69. Answer: A

Explanation: The area of a circle is given by πr^2, so with a radius of 5, the area is 25π square units.

70. Answer: C

Explanation: The Articles of Confederation served as the first constitution of the United States, establishing the first government.

71. Answer: C

Explanation: Capitalism emphasizes individual ownership and the operation of a free market where supply and demand determine prices.

72. Answer: C

Explanation: Igneous rocks are formed from the cooling and solidification of lava or magma.

73. Answer: D

Explanation: The mitochondria are known as the "powerhouses" of the cell, responsible for energy production through cellular respiration.

74. Answer: B

Explanation: Pottery is the art of making objects such as pots, dishes, and other items out of clay.

75. Answer: B

Explanation: Decrescendo, also known as diminuendo, denotes a gradual decrease in volume or intensity in music.

76. Answer: A

Explanation: In physical fitness, "FITT" stands for Frequency, Intensity, Time, and Type. It's a principle used to guide the development of fitness programs.

77. Answer: C

Explanation: Pointillism is a painting technique where small, distinct dots of color are applied in patterns to form an image.

78. Answer: C

Explanation: Fats provide a concentrated source of energy in the diet and help in the absorption and storage of fat-soluble vitamins.

79. Answer: C

Explanation: The climax in drama refers to the point where the conflict reaches its peak or turning point.

80. Answer: C

Explanation: Modern dance often emphasizes personal expression and individual creativity, rather than adhering strictly to traditional forms or narratives.

81. Answer: C

Explanation: Remineralization is the process of adding essential minerals like calcium and magnesium back into water, often after purification.

82. Answer: C

Explanation: Salvador Dalí was a prominent Surrealist artist, known for his imaginative and eccentric works.

83. Answer: B

Explanation: Pilates emphasizes controlled movements, breathing, and alignment to improve flexibility, strength, and balance.

84. Answer: D

Explanation: Realism is an art movement that emphasizes the accurate and truthful depiction of life and objects as they appear in reality.

85. Answer: C

Explanation: A self-examination is a recommended method for individuals to check for lumps or changes in the breast that might indicate cancer. However, it's not a substitute for professional medical screening.

86. Answer: C

Explanation: A mosaic is an art form that involves creating images by arranging small colored pieces of glass, stone, or other materials.

87. Answer: D

Explanation: Calcium is a mineral that is essential for building and maintaining strong bones and teeth.

88. Answer: D

Explanation: Tone refers to the emotional quality or mood conveyed by a work of art, often through the use of color, shading, and other artistic elements.

89. Answer: B

Explanation: Carbohydrates are the body's main source of energy, providing fuel for physical activity and bodily functions.

90. Answer: D

Explanation: Expressionism is an art movement that often uses distorted and exaggerated forms to evoke emotion and create a subjective response from the viewer.

91. Answer: D

Explanation: Dramatic, situational, and verbal irony are recognized types of irony, while "historical irony" is not a recognized category.

92. Answer: A

Explanation: Using the Pythagorean theorem, $a^2+b^2=c^2$, where 6 and 8 are the legs, and c is the hypotenuse, we find that $c=10$.

93. Answer: A

Explanation: George Washington was the first President of the United States under the Constitution, serving from 1789 to 1797.

94. Answer: C

Explanation: Evaporation is the process where a liquid turns into a gas, typically when heated.

95. Answer: B

Explanation: A pirouette is a controlled turn executed on one leg, often making a full 360-degree rotation or more.

96. Answer: B

Explanation: Aerobic exercise primarily helps in improving cardiovascular health by increasing heart rate and improving oxygen circulation.

97. Answer: D

Explanation: Tanka is a form of Japanese poetry consisting of five lines with a syllable pattern of 5, 7, 5, 7, 7.

98. Answer: C

Explanation: 2 is the smallest prime number and the only even prime number.

99. Answer: B

Explanation: Separation of powers is a principle that ensures that no single branch of government has unchecked power, dividing responsibilities among various branches.

100. Answer: B

Explanation: Mars is often referred to as the "Red Planet" due to its reddish appearance, caused by iron oxide, or rust, on its surface.

19.1 Full-Length Practice Test 2

English Language Arts and Reading and the Science of Teaching Reading

Question 101: What literary device is used when non-human objects are given human characteristics?
A) Metaphor
B) Simile
C) Personification
D) Hyperbole

Mathematics

Question 102: If a circle has a diameter of 14, what is its area?
A) 49π
B) 154π
C) 196π
D) 78π

Social Studies

Question 103: What 19th-century policy aimed to make Native American tribes assimilate into European-American culture?

A) Manifest Destiny

B) Indian Removal Act

C) Dawes Act

D) Monroe Doctrine

Science

Question 104: What is the primary function of the chloroplasts in a plant cell?

A) Reproduction

B) Photosynthesis

C) Respiration

D) Digestion

Fine Arts, Health, and Physical Education

Question 105: What style of painting aims to represent objects without reference to visual or emotional reality?

A) Abstract

B) Impressionism

C) Surrealism

D) Realism

English Language Arts and Reading and the Science of Teaching Reading

Question 106: In writing, what term refers to the conclusion of a story where all loose ends are tied up?

A) Climax

B) Denouement

C) Protagonist

D) Foreshadowing

Mathematics

Question 107: What is the slope of the line defined by the equation $y=-3x+4$?

A) -3

B) 4

C) 0

D) 3

Social Studies

Question 108: Which U.S. President implemented the New Deal during the Great Depression?

A) Herbert Hoover

B) Franklin D. Roosevelt

C) Theodore Roosevelt

D) Harry S. Truman

Science

Question 109: What type of rock is formed by the cooling of molten magma?

A) Metamorphic

B) Sedimentary

C) Igneous

D) Limestone

Fine Arts, Health, and Physical Education

Question 110: In music, what symbol indicates that a note should be played one-half step lower?
A) Sharp
B) Flat
C) Natural
D) Crescendo

English Language Arts and Reading and the Science of Teaching Reading

Question 111: What type of conflict occurs between a character and an external force, such as nature or society?
A) Man vs. Self
B) Man vs. Man
C) Man vs. Society
D) Man vs. Nature

Mathematics

Question 112: What is the sum of the interior angles of a pentagon?
A) 540°
B) 720°
C) 900°
D) 1080°

Social Studies

Question 113: What philosophical movement emphasized reason, individualism, and skepticism of tradition during the 17th and 18th centuries?
A) Existentialism

B) Romanticism

C) Enlightenment

D) Modernism

Science

Question 114: Which planet in our solar system has the strongest magnetic field?

A) Earth

B) Jupiter

C) Mars

D) Saturn

Fine Arts, Health, and Physical Education

Question 115: What is the practice of controlling the breath to enhance mental clarity and wellness called?

A) Meditation

B) Aerobics

C) Pilates

D) Pranayama

English Language Arts and Reading and the Science of Teaching Reading

Question 116: Which of the following is an example of onomatopoeia?

A) The sun smiled down on the garden.

B) The cat's meow echoed in the night.

C) The wind howled through the trees.

D) Her smile was as bright as the sun.

Mathematics

Question 117: If $f(x)=2x+3$, what is the value of $f(4)$?
A) 5
B) 8
C) 11
D) 19

Social Studies

Question 118: Which African country was never colonized during the European Scramble for Africa?
A) South Africa
B) Nigeria
C) Ethiopia
D) Kenya

Science

Question 119: Which element is classified as a Noble Gas?
A) Oxygen
B) Hydrogen
C) Helium
D) Carbon

Fine Arts, Health, and Physical Education

Question 120: What type of theatrical production involves singing, acting, and dancing, often telling a story through songs?
A) Tragedy

B) Drama

C) Musical

D) Comedy

English Language Arts and Reading and the Science of Teaching Reading

Question 121: What is the term for a brief story used to illustrate a moral or spiritual lesson, often attributed to Jesus in the New Testament?

A) Fable

B) Parable

C) Allegory

D) Metaphor

Mathematics

Question 122: What is the probability of rolling a 3 on a standard six-sided die?

A) 1/3

B) 1/6

C) 1/2

D) 2/3

Social Studies

Question 123: What was the main reason for the establishment of the United Nations?

A) To promote free trade

B) To encourage global tourism

C) To maintain international peace and security

D) To enforce international law

Science

Question 124: What type of bond is formed when electrons are shared between atoms?
A) Ionic
B) Covalent
C) Metallic
D) Hydrogen

Fine Arts, Health, and Physical Education

Question 125: What does the term "allegro" mean in musical notation?
A) Slowly
B) Loudly
C) Quickly
D) Softly

English Language Arts and Reading and the Science of Teaching Reading

Question 126: Which literary term refers to the central message or lesson of a literary work?
A) Theme
B) Tone
C) Mood
D) Setting

Mathematics

Question 127: If $f(x)=3x^2-2x+5$, what is the value of $f(-1)$?

A) 10

B) 0

C) 8

D) -10

Social Studies

Question 128: Who was the first woman to fly solo across the Atlantic Ocean?

A) Bessie Coleman

B) Amelia Earhart

C) Sally Ride

D) Valentina Tereshkova

Science

Question 129: What process do plants use to release oxygen and produce glucose from carbon dioxide and water?

A) Cellular respiration

B) Fermentation

C) Photosynthesis

D) Digestion

Fine Arts, Health, and Physical Education

Question 130: In dance, what term is used to describe a complete turn on one foot?

A) Plie

B) Pirouette

C) Arabesque

D) Jete

English Language Arts and Reading and the Science of Teaching Reading

Question 131: What type of sentence structure contains two independent clauses joined by a coordinating conjunction?

A) Compound sentence

B) Complex sentence

C) Simple sentence

D) Fragment

Mathematics

Question 132: What is the midpoint of the line segment with endpoints at (2, 3) and (8, 7)?

A) (5, 5)

B) (4, 4)

C) (3, 2)

D) (6, 6)

Social Studies

Question 133: Which constitutional amendment abolished slavery in the United States?

A) 13th Amendment

B) 15th Amendment

C) 19th Amendment

D) 21st Amendment

Science

Question 134: What is the atomic number of carbon?
A) 6
B) 12
C) 14
D) 8

Fine Arts, Health, and Physical Education

Question 135: What is the term for a dramatic, often improvised performance in which performers explore roles, situations, or dramatic themes?
A) Soliloquy
B) Monologue
C) Dialogue
D) Improvisation

English Language Arts and Reading and the Science of Teaching Reading

Question 136: In literature, what is the opposite of a protagonist?
A) Antagonist
B) Sidekick
C) Narrator
D) Foil

Mathematics

Question 137: How many distinct triangles can be formed with sides of lengths 3, 4, and 5?

A) 0

B) 1

C) 2

D) 3

Social Studies

Question 138: What was the primary economic system in medieval Europe?

A) Capitalism

B) Socialism

C) Mercantilism

D) Feudalism

Science

Question 139: What organelle is responsible for energy production in the form of ATP within a cell?

A) Ribosome

B) Mitochondria

C) Chloroplast

D) Golgi Apparatus

Fine Arts, Health, and Physical Education

Question 140: What is the term for the visual appearance or style of a work of art?

A) Composition

B) Aesthetic

C) Technique

D) Medium

English Language Arts and Reading and the Science of Teaching Reading

Question 141: What is the primary purpose of an expository essay?
A) To entertain
B) To persuade
C) To inform
D) To describe

Mathematics

Question 142: What is the sum of the interior angles of a hexagon?
A) 540°
B) 720°
C) 180°
D) 900°

Social Studies

Question 143: Who was the leader of the Soviet Union during the Cuban Missile Crisis?
A) Leon Trotsky
B) Nikita Khrushchev
C) Vladimir Lenin
D) Joseph Stalin

Science

Question 144: What phase of matter has a definite volume but no definite shape?

A) Solid

B) Liquid

C) Gas

D) Plasma

Fine Arts, Health, and Physical Education

Question 145: Which musical notation symbol indicates a note's duration should be lengthened by half its value?

A) Fermata

B) Staccato

C) Dot

D) Tie

English Language Arts and Reading and the Science of Teaching Reading

Question 146: What literary device involves a play on words, often employing multiple meanings or similar-sounding words?

A) Simile

B) Pun

C) Onomatopoeia

D) Hyperbole

Mathematics

Question 147: What is the solution to the equation $2x-5=11$?

A) $x=3$

B) $x=8$

C) $x=-3$
D) $x=5$

Social Studies

Question 148: What was the main purpose of the Marshall Plan after World War II?
A) To rebuild and stabilize Western European economies
B) To promote communism in Eastern Europe
C) To establish military bases in Asia
D) To support dictatorships in South America

Science

Question 149: What is the common name for the plant species "Helianthus annuus"?
A) Rose
B) Tulip
C) Sunflower
D) Daisy

Fine Arts, Health, and Physical Education

Question 150: In ballet, what term refers to a high, vertical jump in which one leg extends forward and the other backward?
A) Arabesque
B) Grand Jeté
C) Plie
D) Pirouette

English Language Arts and Reading and the Science of Teaching Reading

Question 151: What is the main function of a thesis statement in an essay?
A) To provide evidence
B) To summarize the conclusion
C) To state the main idea or argument
D) To create a hook for the reader

Mathematics

Question 152: What is the solution to the equation $5x-3=2x+4$?
A) $x=7/3$
B) $x=-1$
C) $x=5/3$
D) $x=1$

Social Studies

Question 153: Who was the first President of the United States?
A) Thomas Jefferson
B) George Washington
C) John Adams
D) Benjamin Franklin

Science

Question 154: Which layer of Earth's atmosphere contains the ozone layer?
A) Troposphere
B) Stratosphere

C) Mesosphere

D) Thermosphere

Fine Arts, Health, and Physical Education

Question 155: What type of paint is made by mixing pigment with water-soluble binder medium, such as egg yolk?

A) Oil paint

B) Acrylic paint

C) Watercolor paint

D) Tempera paint

English Language Arts and Reading and the Science of Teaching Reading

Question 156: Which type of narration uses pronouns like "he," "she," or "they" and provides insight into only one character's thoughts and feelings?

A) First person

B) Third person limited

C) Third person omniscient

D) Second person

Mathematics

Question 157: What is the volume of a cylinder with radius 4 cm and height 10 cm? (Use $\pi=3.14$)

A) 160 cm³

B) 502.4 cm³

C) 125.6 cm³

D) 314 cm³

Social Studies

Question 158: What economic system emphasizes collective or governmental ownership and administration of the means of production and distribution of goods?
A) Capitalism
B) Socialism
C) Mercantilism
D) Feudalism

Science

Question 159: Which element is a Noble Gas with an atomic number of 10?
A) Helium
B) Oxygen
C) Neon
D) Argon

Fine Arts, Health, and Physical Education

Question 160: What are the basic rhythmic units in a musical composition called?
A) Chords
B) Measures
C) Beats
D) Bars

English Language Arts and Reading and the Science of Teaching Reading

Question 161: What type of figurative language uses "like" or "as" to make a direct comparison between two things?

A) Simile

B) Metaphor

C) Hyperbole

D) Onomatopoeia

Mathematics

Question 162: If a triangle has angles measuring 30°, 60°, and 90°, what type of triangle is it?

A) Equilateral

B) Isosceles

C) Scalene

D) Right

Social Studies

Question 163: Which historical event marked the beginning of the modern civil rights movement in the United States?

A) Emancipation Proclamation

B) Montgomery Bus Boycott

C) Brown vs. Board of Education decision

D) Martin Luther King Jr.'s "I Have a Dream" speech

Science

Question 164: Which organelle is found in plant cells but not in animal cells?

A) Mitochondria

B) Ribosome

C) Chloroplast

D) Nucleus

Fine Arts, Health, and Physical Education

Question 165: In drama, what term refers to the spoken part of a play, as distinct from songs, music, or dance?

A) Dialogue

B) Monologue

C) Script

D) Libretto

English Language Arts and Reading and the Science of Teaching Reading

Question 166: What is the act of providing a detailed analysis or interpretation of a literary work called?

A) Summarization

B) Criticism

C) Symbolism

D) Annotation

Mathematics

Question 167: What is the probability of rolling a 3 with a standard six-sided die?

A) 1/3

B) 1/6

C) 1/2

D) 2/3

Social Studies

Question 168: What was the primary purpose of the Berlin Wall?
A) To protect West Berlin from military invasion
B) To separate East and West Germany
C) To keep East Germans from escaping to West Berlin
D) To mark the boundary between NATO and Warsaw Pact countries

Science

Question 169: What type of biome is characterized by cold temperatures, low precipitation, and permafrost?
A) Tundra
B) Desert
C) Rainforest
D) Temperate Forest

Fine Arts, Health, and Physical Education

Question 170: In music, what term refers to a composition for a solo instrument or voice?
A) Symphony
B) Sonata
C) Chorus
D) Ensemble

English Language Arts and Reading and the Science of Teaching Reading

Question 171: What is the term for the leading character or one of the major characters in a play, film, novel, etc.?

A) Antagonist

B) Protagonist

C) Foil

D) Mentor

Mathematics

Question 172: What is the area of a circle with a radius of 5 cm? (Use $\pi=3.14$)

A) 15.7 cm²

B) 31.4 cm²

C) 78.5 cm²

D) 157 cm²

Social Studies

Question 173: What treaty ended the Revolutionary War between the United States and Britain?

A) Treaty of Ghent

B) Treaty of Versailles

C) Treaty of Tordesillas

D) Treaty of Paris

Science

Question 174: What is the process by which plants convert sunlight, carbon dioxide, and water into glucose and oxygen?

A) Respiration

B) Digestion

C) Photosynthesis

D) Fermentation

Fine Arts, Health, and Physical Education

Question 175: Which art movement emphasized the rejection of traditional artistic styles and the celebration of modern technology and industrialization?

A) Romanticism

B) Cubism

C) Futurism

D) Impressionism

English Language Arts and Reading and the Science of Teaching Reading

Question 176: What literary device uses an object or action to mean something more than its literal meaning?

A) Irony

B) Alliteration

C) Symbolism

D) Onomatopoeia

Mathematics

Question 177: What is the solution to the equation $2x+4=12$?

A) 2

B) 4

C) 3

D) 6

Social Studies

Question 178: Which U.S. President signed the Emancipation Proclamation?

A) Thomas Jefferson

B) Abraham Lincoln

C) Andrew Jackson

D) George Washington

Science

Question 179: What is the atomic number of hydrogen?

A) 1

B) 2

C) 3

D) 4

Fine Arts, Health, and Physical Education

Question 180: In dance, what is the term for a turn on one foot that is usually executed on pointe or demi-pointe?

A) Pirouette

B) Plie

C) Arabesque

D) Jeté

English Language Arts and Reading and the Science of Teaching Reading

Question 181: What is the structural framework that underlies the order and manner in which a narrative is presented to a reader?

A) Tone
B) Plot
C) Theme
D) Setting

Mathematics

Question 182: If a triangle has angles measuring 45°, 45°, and 90°, what type of triangle is it?
A) Equilateral
B) Scalene
C) Isosceles
D) Obtuse

Social Studies

Question 183: What economic system emphasizes collective ownership of the means of production?
A) Capitalism
B) Socialism
C) Mercantilism
D) Feudalism

Science

Question 184: What type of rock is formed from the cooling and solidification of magma or lava?
A) Sedimentary
B) Metamorphic

C) Igneous

D) Mineral

Fine Arts, Health, and Physical Education

Question 185: What does the musical term "adagio" mean?

A) Fast

B) Loud

C) Slow

D) Soft

English Language Arts and Reading and the Science of Teaching Reading

Question 186: In literature, what is the antagonist's role?

A) To support the protagonist

B) To oppose the protagonist

C) To narrate the story

D) To provide comic relief

Mathematics

Question 187: What is the sum of the interior angles of a rectangle?

A) 540°

B) 360°

C) 180°

D) 720°

Social Studies

Question 188: What was the Marshall Plan designed to do?

A) Rebuild European economies after World War II

B) Provide military aid to South Vietnam

C) Establish a peace treaty with the Soviet Union

D) Promote U.S. businesses during the Great Depression

Science

Question 189: What phase change occurs when a solid turns directly into a gas without passing through the liquid phase?

A) Melting

B) Freezing

C) Sublimation

D) Condensation

Fine Arts, Health, and Physical Education

Question 190: What art style focuses on abstract elements like shapes, colors, lines, and forms?

A) Realism

B) Cubism

C) Surrealism

D) Impressionism

English Language Arts and Reading and the Science of Teaching Reading

Question 191: What is the main purpose of a thesis statement in an essay?

A) To summarize the conclusion

B) To list the sources

C) To state the main idea or argument

D) To provide an interesting anecdote

Mathematics

Question 192: A car travels 60 miles in 2 hours. What is its average speed?

A) 30 miles per hour

B) 60 miles per hour

C) 20 miles per hour

D) 120 miles per hour

Social Studies

Question 193: What ancient civilization is known for its hieroglyphic writing and pyramids?

A) Mesopotamia

B) Greece

C) Rome

D) Egypt

Science

Question 194: What is the process by which plants convert sunlight, carbon dioxide, and water into glucose and oxygen?

A) Respiration

B) Photosynthesis

C) Digestion

D) Fermentation

Fine Arts, Health, and Physical Education

Question 195: Which of the following is a key component of physical fitness related to the ability of the heart, lungs, and blood vessels to supply oxygen to working muscles during physical activity?

A) Flexibility

B) Muscular strength

C) Cardiovascular endurance

D) Balance

English Language Arts and Reading and the Science of Teaching Reading

Question 196: What is a literary term for a brief and indirect reference to a person, place, thing, or idea of historical, cultural, literary, or political significance that is not elaborated on?

A) Metaphor

B) Simile

C) Allusion

D) Hyperbole

Mathematics

Question 197: If the radius of a circle is 5 cm, what is its circumference? (Use $\pi=3.14$)

A) 10 cm

B) 31.4 cm

C) 15.7 cm

D) 78.5 cm

Social Studies

Question 198: Who wrote "The Communist Manifesto"?

A) Thomas Hobbes

B) John Locke

C) Karl Marx and Friedrich Engels

D) Adam Smith

Science

Question 199: What is the most abundant gas in Earth's atmosphere?

A) Oxygen

B) Carbon Dioxide

C) Nitrogen

D) Argon

Fine Arts, Health, and Physical Education

Question 200: In music, what is the term used to describe a gradual increase in loudness?

A) Crescendo

B) Forte

C) Allegro

D) Diminuendo

19.2 ANSWER SHEET - PRACTICE TEST 2

101. Answer: C

Explanation: Personification is a literary device where non-human objects are given human characteristics or emotions.

102. Answer: A

Explanation: The radius of the circle is half the diameter, or 7. The area of a circle is given by $A=\pi r^2$, so the area is 49π.

103. Answer: C

Explanation: The Dawes Act aimed to assimilate Native American tribes into European-American culture by breaking up reservations and allocating land to individual households.

104. Answer: B

Explanation: The primary function of chloroplasts in a plant cell is photosynthesis, the process of converting light energy into glucose.

105. Answer: A

Explanation: Abstract art aims to represent objects without reference to visual or emotional reality, focusing on shapes, colors, and forms.

106. Answer: B

Explanation: The denouement is the conclusion of a story where all the loose ends are tied up, following the climax.

107. Answer: A

Explanation: In the slope-intercept form $y=mx+b$, the slope is represented by m. In this case, the slope is -3.

108. Answer: B

Explanation: Franklin D. Roosevelt implemented the New Deal to address the economic challenges of the Great Depression.

109. Answer: C

Explanation: Igneous rock is formed by the cooling and solidification of molten magma or lava.

110. Answer: B

Explanation: A flat symbol in music indicates that a note should be played one-half step lower.

111. Answer: C

Explanation: Man vs. Society conflict occurs when a character faces opposition or pressure from societal norms or laws.

112. Answer: A

Explanation: The sum of the interior angles of a polygon with n sides is given by $(n-2)\times 180°$. For a pentagon, $n=5$, so the sum is 540°.

113. Answer: C

Explanation: The Enlightenment emphasized reason, individualism, and skepticism of tradition during the 17th and 18th centuries.

114. Answer: B

Explanation: Jupiter has the strongest magnetic field of any planet in our solar system.

115. Answer: D

Explanation: Pranayama is the practice of breath control in yoga, used to enhance mental clarity and wellness.

116. Answer: C

Explanation: Onomatopoeia is a word that imitates the sound it represents. In this case, "howled" is an example of onomatopoeia.

117. Answer: C

Explanation: Substituting $x=4$ into the equation gives $f(4)=2·4+3=8+3=11$.

118. Answer: C

Explanation: Ethiopia was never formally colonized by European powers during the Scramble for Africa.

119. Answer: C

Explanation: Helium is classified as a Noble Gas, known for its low reactivity.

120. Answer: C

Explanation: A musical is a type of theatrical production that combines singing, acting, and dancing, often telling a story through songs.

121. Answer: B

Explanation: A parable is a brief story used to illustrate a moral or spiritual lesson, often found in the teachings of Jesus in the New Testament.

122. Answer: B

Explanation: Since there is only one way to roll a 3 on a six-sided die, the probability is 1/6.

123. Answer: C

Explanation: The main reason for the establishment of the United Nations was to maintain international peace and security.

124. Answer: B

Explanation: Covalent bonds are formed when electrons are shared between atoms, creating a strong link between them.

125. Answer: C

Explanation: In musical notation, "allegro" is an instruction to play quickly and lively.

126. Answer: A

Explanation: The theme is the central message or lesson that a literary work conveys.

127. Answer: A

Explanation: Substituting $x=-1$ into the equation, we have $f(-1)=3(-1)2-2(-1)+5=3+2+5=10$.

128. Answer: B

Explanation: Amelia Earhart was the first woman to fly solo across the Atlantic Ocean in 1932.

129. Answer: C

Explanation: Photosynthesis is the process by which plants convert carbon dioxide and water into glucose and release oxygen.

130. Answer: B

Explanation: A pirouette is a complete turn on one foot in dance.

131. Answer: A

Explanation: A compound sentence contains two independent clauses that are joined by a coordinating conjunction.

132. Answer: A

Explanation: The midpoint of a line segment is given by $(x1+x2/2, y1+y2/2)$. In this case, the midpoint is $(2+8/2, 3+7/2)=(5,5)$.

133. Answer: A

Explanation: The 13th Amendment to the U.S. Constitution abolished slavery.

134. Answer: A

Explanation: The atomic number of carbon, representing the number of protons in the nucleus, is 6.

135. Answer: D

Explanation: Improvisation is a dramatic, often spontaneous performance in which performers explore roles, situations, or dramatic themes without a script.

136. Answer: A

Explanation: The antagonist is typically the character who opposes the protagonist or main character in a story.

137. Answer: B

Explanation: Only one distinct triangle can be formed with sides of lengths 3, 4, and 5, as these lengths satisfy the triangle inequality theorem.

138. Answer: D

Explanation: Feudalism was the primary economic system in medieval Europe, characterized by the hierarchical relationship between lords and vassals.

139. Answer: B

Explanation: The mitochondria are responsible for energy production in the form of ATP within a cell.

140. Answer: B

Explanation: The term "aesthetic" refers to the visual appearance or style of a work of art.

141. Answer: C

Explanation: The primary purpose of an expository essay is to inform or explain a topic to the reader.

142. Answer: B

Explanation: The sum of the interior angles of a hexagon with n sides is given by $(n-2)\times 180°$. For a hexagon, $n=6$, so the sum is $720°$.

143. Answer: B

Explanation: Nikita Khrushchev was the leader of the Soviet Union during the Cuban Missile Crisis in 1962.

144. Answer: B

Explanation: Liquids have a definite volume but no definite shape, as they take the shape of their container.

145. Answer: C

Explanation: A dot placed to the right of a note in musical notation indicates that the note's duration should be lengthened by half its value.

146. Answer: B

Explanation: A pun is a play on words that exploits multiple meanings or similar-sounding words for humorous or rhetorical effect.

147. Answer: B

Explanation: Solving for x, we have $2x=16$, so $x=8$.

148. Answer: A

Explanation: The main purpose of the Marshall Plan was to rebuild and stabilize Western European economies after World War II.

149. Answer: C

Explanation: "Helianthus annuus" is the scientific name for the sunflower.

150. Answer: B

Explanation: In ballet, a Grand Jeté is a high, vertical jump in which one leg extends forward and the other backward.

151. Answer: C

Explanation: A thesis statement clearly states the main idea or argument of an essay.

152. Answer: A

Explanation: By moving all the terms to one side, we get $3x=7$, so $x=7/3$.

153. Answer: B

Explanation: George Washington was the first President of the United States.

154. Answer: B

Explanation: The ozone layer is found in the stratosphere.

155. Answer: D

Explanation: Tempera paint is made by mixing pigment with a water-soluble binder like egg yolk.

156. Answer: B

Explanation: Third person limited narration uses pronouns like "he," "she," or "they" and provides insight into only one character's thoughts and feelings.

157. Answer: B

Explanation: The volume of a cylinder is given by $\pi r^2 h$, so the volume is $3.14 \times 4^2 \times 10 = 502.4 \, cm^3$.

158. Answer: B

Explanation: Socialism emphasizes collective or governmental ownership and administration of the means of production and distribution of goods.

159. Answer: C

Explanation: Neon is a Noble Gas and has an atomic number of 10.

160. Answer: C

Explanation: The basic rhythmic units in a musical composition are called beats.

161. Answer: A

Explanation: A simile uses "like" or "as" to make a direct comparison between two things.

162. Answer: D

Explanation: A triangle with angles measuring 30°, 60°, and 90° is a right triangle.

163. Answer: C

Explanation: The Brown vs. Board of Education decision marked the beginning of the modern civil rights movement in the United States.

164. Answer: C

Explanation: Chloroplasts are found in plant cells but not in animal cells.

165. Answer: A

Explanation: Dialogue refers to the spoken part of a play, as distinct from songs, music, or dance.

166. Answer: B

Explanation: Criticism is the act of providing a detailed analysis or interpretation of a literary work.

167. Answer: B

Explanation: The probability of rolling a specific number with a standard six-sided die is 1/6.

168. Answer: C

Explanation: The primary purpose of the Berlin Wall was to keep East Germans from escaping to West Berlin.

169. Answer: A

Explanation: The tundra biome is characterized by cold temperatures, low precipitation, and permafrost.

170. Answer: B

Explanation: A sonata is a composition for a solo instrument or voice.

171. Answer: B

Explanation: The protagonist is the leading character or one of the major characters in a work of literature.

172. Answer: C

Explanation: The area of a circle is given by πr^2, so the area is $3.14 \times 5^2 = 78.5 \, cm^2$.

173. Answer: D

Explanation: The Treaty of Paris ended the Revolutionary War between the United States and Britain.

174. Answer: C

Explanation: Photosynthesis is the process by which plants convert sunlight, carbon dioxide, and water into glucose and oxygen.

175. Answer: C

Explanation: Futurism emphasized the rejection of traditional artistic styles and the celebration of modern technology and industrialization.

176. Answer: C

Explanation: Symbolism uses an object or action to represent something more than its literal meaning.

177. Answer: B

Explanation: To find the value of x, subtract 4 from both sides and then divide by 2: $2x=8$, so $x=4$.

178. Answer: B

Explanation: President Abraham Lincoln signed the Emancipation Proclamation in 1863.

179. Answer: A

Explanation: The atomic number of hydrogen is 1, meaning it has one proton in its nucleus.

180. Answer: A

Explanation: A pirouette is a turn on one foot, usually executed on pointe or demi-pointe.

181. Answer: B

Explanation: Plot is the structural framework that underlies the order and manner in which a narrative is presented.

182. Answer: C

Explanation: An isosceles triangle has two angles that are the same, so a triangle with angles measuring 45°, 45°, and 90° is an isosceles triangle.

183. Answer: B

Explanation: Socialism emphasizes collective ownership of the means of production.

184. Answer: C

Explanation: Igneous rock is formed from the cooling and solidification of magma or lava.

185. Answer: C

Explanation: "Adagio" is a musical term that means slow.

186. Answer: B

Explanation: The antagonist's role in literature is to oppose the protagonist.

187. Answer: B

Explanation: The sum of the interior angles of a rectangle with n sides is given by $(n-2)\times 180°$. For a rectangle, $n=4$, so the sum is $(4-2)\times 180°=360°$.

188. Answer: A

Explanation: The Marshall Plan was designed to rebuild European economies after World War II.

189. Answer: C

Explanation: Sublimation is the phase change in which a solid turns directly into a gas without passing through the liquid phase.

190. Answer: B

Explanation: Cubism is an art style that focuses on abstract elements like shapes, colors, lines, and forms.

191. Answer: C

Explanation: The main purpose of a thesis statement in an essay is to state the main idea or argument.

192. Answer: A

Explanation: The average speed is found by dividing the total distance by the total time: 60 miles/2 hours=30 miles per hour.

193. Answer: D

Explanation: Ancient Egypt is known for its hieroglyphic writing and pyramids.

194. Answer: B

Explanation: Photosynthesis is the process by which plants convert sunlight, carbon dioxide, and water into glucose and oxygen.

195. Answer: C

Explanation: Cardiovascular endurance is related to the ability of the heart, lungs, and blood vessels to supply oxygen to working muscles during physical activity.

196. Answer: C

Explanation: An allusion is a brief and indirect reference to a significant person, place, thing, or idea that is not elaborated on.

197. Answer: B

Explanation: The circumference of a circle is given by $2\pi r$, so for a radius of 5 cm, the circumference is 2×3.14×5=31.4 cm.

198. Answer: C

Explanation: "The Communist Manifesto" was written by Karl Marx and Friedrich Engels.

199. Answer: C

Explanation: Nitrogen is the most abundant gas in Earth's atmosphere, making up about 78% of the atmosphere.

200. Answer: A

Explanation: Crescendo is the term used to describe a gradual increase in loudness in music.

Test-Taking Strategies

Navigating the TExES exam requires not only knowledge but also effective test-taking strategies and the ability to manage test anxiety. In this section, we equip you with a toolkit of strategies to approach the exam with confidence, conquer your nerves, and showcase your true capabilities.

1. Read the Instructions Thoroughly:
Before diving into the questions, take a moment to read the instructions for each section carefully. Understanding the format, time limits, and question types ensures that you're well-prepared to tackle the exam.

2. Manage Your Time Wisely:
Time management is crucial. Allocate a specific amount of time for each question or section and stick to it. If you encounter a challenging question, make a note and move on. Return to it after completing the easier questions.

3. Understand Question Patterns:
Familiarize yourself with common question patterns, such as multiple-choice, constructed-response, and teaching simulations. Practice with different question types to build familiarity and develop efficient strategies.

4. Process of Elimination:
When faced with multiple-choice questions, use the process of elimination to narrow down your choices. Eliminate obviously incorrect answers and then evaluate the remaining options.

5. Keyword Analysis:

Pay close attention to keywords in the questions. Keywords often provide clues about what is being asked or the context of the question. Analyzing keywords can guide you to the correct answer.

6. Constructed-Response Clarity:

For constructed-response questions, structure your answers clearly and concisely. Use bullet points or organized paragraphs to communicate your thoughts effectively.

7. Teaching Simulations:

In teaching simulations, apply classroom management strategies, instructional techniques, and student engagement practices you've learned. Utilize real-world experiences and draw from your knowledge to craft comprehensive solutions.

8. Positive Self-Talk:

Replace negative self-talk with positive affirmations. Remind yourself of your preparation, knowledge, and capabilities. Believing in your abilities boosts your confidence and minimizes test anxiety.

9. Breathing Techniques:

Combat test anxiety with deep breathing techniques. Practice deep, slow breaths to calm your nerves and focus your mind. Taking deliberate breaths before and during the exam can enhance your clarity and concentration.

10. Visualize Success:

Visualize yourself succeeding in the exam. Picture yourself answering questions confidently and navigating challenging scenarios with ease. Visualization can enhance your confidence and reduce anxiety.

11. Take Breaks:

During the exam, take short breaks if allowed. Stand up, stretch, and take a few deep breaths to refresh your mind and release tension. Returning to the test with a clear mind can improve your performance.

Remember that test-taking strategies are as crucial as content knowledge. By implementing these strategies, you're not only enhancing your chances of success but also developing skills that will serve you well in your future teaching career. Tackle the TExES exam with a strategic mindset, confident approach, and the assurance that you've prepared diligently.

ADDITIONAL RESOURCES

As you embark on your journey to conquer the TExES exam, we understand the importance of having a well-rounded toolkit of resources at your disposal. In addition to the comprehensive content provided in this book, we recommend exploring the following online resources and academic materials to enhance your preparation and further solidify your understanding.

Recommended Online Resources:

1. **Texas Education Agency (TEA) Website:** The official TEA website offers a wealth of information about the TExES exam, including registration details, test descriptions, and updates. Stay connected to official announcements and resources.

2. **Educator Certification Online System (ECOS):** ECOS allows you to manage your educator certification account, register for exams, and access score reports. It's an essential platform for candidates seeking certification in Texas.

3. **Online Practice Test Providers:** Utilize reputable online platforms that offer TExES practice tests. These tests simulate the actual exam environment, allowing you to assess your readiness and familiarize yourself with question types.

4. **Educational Blogs and Forums:** Engage with educator-focused blogs

and forums where professionals and candidates share their experiences, strategies, and insights about the TExES exam. Participating in discussions can offer additional perspectives and advice.

5. **Educational YouTube Channels:** Explore educational YouTube channels that provide tutorials, explanations, and tips related to the TExES exam content. Visual explanations can enhance your understanding of complex topics.

Recommended Academic Materials:

1. **TExES Preparation Guides:** Look for reputable TExES exam preparation guides that complement your study plan. These guides often provide additional practice questions, content explanations, and test-taking strategies.

2. **Educational Reference Books:** Invest in reference books related to the core subjects tested in the TExES exam. These books offer in-depth explanations and additional examples to supplement your understanding.

3. **Subject-Specific Textbooks:** If you need to delve deeper into specific subject areas, consider using subject-specific textbooks used in education programs. These resources offer comprehensive coverage of content.

4. **Academic Journals and Research Papers:** For educators who wish to explore advanced concepts, academic journals and research papers in education provide insights into current trends, teaching methodologies, and best practices.

5. **Professional Development Workshops:** Attend workshops and seminars offered by educational organizations and institutions. These events provide opportunities for hands-on learning, networking, and staying

up-to-date with educational trends.

By integrating these recommended online resources and academic materials into your preparation strategy, you can further enrich your understanding of the TExES exam content and gain insights from a variety of perspectives. Remember that a diverse range of resources can enhance your learning experience and contribute to your success as an educator.

EXPLORE OUR RANGE OF STUDY GUIDES

At Test Treasure Publication, we understand that academic success requires more than just raw intelligence or tireless effort—it requires targeted preparation. That's why we offer an extensive range of study guides, meticulously designed to help you excel in various exams across the USA.

Our Offerings

- **Medical Exams:** Conquer the MCAT, USMLE, and more with our comprehensive study guides, complete with practice questions and diagnostic tests.

- **Law Exams:** Get a leg up on the LSAT and bar exams with our tailored resources, offering theoretical insights and practical exercises.

- **Business and Management Tests:** Ace the GMAT and other business exams with our incisive guides, equipped with real-world examples and scenarios.

- **Engineering & Technical Exams:** Prep for the FE, PE, and other technical exams with our specialized guides, which delve into both fundamentals and complexities.

- **High School Exams:** Be it the SAT, ACT, or AP tests, our high school range is designed to give you a competitive edge.

- **State-Specific Exams:** Tailored resources to help you with exams unique to specific states, whether it's teacher qualification exams or state civil service exams.

Why Choose Test Treasure Publication?

- **Comprehensive Coverage:** Each guide covers all essential topics in detail.

- **Quality Material:** Crafted by experts in each field.

- **Interactive Tools:** Flashcards, online quizzes, and downloadable resources to complement your study.

- **Customizable Learning:** Personalize your prep journey by focusing on areas where you need the most help.

- **Community Support:** Access to online forums where you can discuss concerns, seek guidance, and share success stories.

Contact Us

For inquiries about our study guides, or to provide feedback, please email us at support@testtreasure.com.

Order Now

Ready to elevate your preparation to the next level? Visit our website www.testtreasure.com to browse our complete range of study guides and make your purchase.

Made in the USA
Coppell, TX
23 February 2025